Tacitus *Histories* I

The following titles are available from Bloomsbury for the OCR specifications in Latin and Greek for examinations from June 2019 to June 2021

Apuleius *Metamorphoses* V: A Selection, with introduction, commentary notes and vocabulary by Stuart R. Thomson

Cicero *Philippic* II: A Selection, with introduction, commentary notes and vocabulary by Christopher Tanfield

Horace *Odes*: A Selection, with introduction, commentary notes and vocabulary by John Godwin

Horace *Satires*: A Selection, with introduction, commentary notes and vocabulary by John Godwin

Ovid *Amores* II: A Selection, with introduction, commentary notes and vocabulary by Alfred Artley

Tacitus *Histories* I: A Selection, with introduction by Ellen O'Gorman and commentary notes and vocabulary by Benedict Gravell

Virgil *Aeneid* XI: A Selection, with introduction, commentary notes and vocabulary by Ashley Carter

OCR Anthology for Classical Greek AS and A Level, covering the prescribed texts by Aristophanes, Euripides, Herodotus, Homer, Plato and Xenophon, with introduction, commentary notes and vocabulary by Stephen P. Anderson, Rob Colborn, Neil Croally, Charlie Paterson, Chris Tudor and Claire Webster

Supplementary resources for these volumes can be found at www.bloomsbury.com/OCR-editions–2019–2021

Please type the URL into your web browser and follow the instructions to access the Companion Website. If you experience any problems, please contact Bloomsbury at academicwebsite@bloomsbury.com

Tacitus *Histories* I:
A Selection

Chapters 4–7, 12–14, 17–23, 26, 27–36, 39–44, 49

With introduction by Ellen O'Gorman
and commentary notes and vocabulary
by Benedict Gravell

BLOOMSBURY ACADEMIC
LONDON · NEW YORK · OXFORD · NEW DELHI · SYDNEY

BLOOMSBURY ACADEMIC
Bloomsbury Publishing Plc
50 Bedford Square, London, WC1B 3DP, UK

BLOOMSBURY, BLOOMSBURY ACADEMIC and the Diana logo are trademarks of
Bloomsbury Publishing Plc

First published in Great Britain 2018

Cover image: Bildarchiv Monheim GmbH / Alamy Stock Photo

Library of Congress Cataloging-in-Publication Data
Names: Tacitus, Cornelius, author. | O'Gorman, Ellen, writer of introduction. |
Gravell, Benedict, writer of added commentary.
Title: Histories I : a selection : 4–7, 12–14, 17–23, 26, 27–36, 39–44, 49 / Tacitus ; with
introduction by Ellen O'Gorman and commentary notes and vocabulary by Benedict Gravell.
Description: London ; New York : Bloomsbury Academic, an imprint of
Bloomsbury Publishing Plc, 2018. | In Latin; introduction and commentary in English. |
Includes bibliographical references.
Identifiers: LCCN 2017049946| ISBN 9781350010154 (pbk.) | ISBN 9781350010185 (epdf)
Subjects: LCSH: Tacitus, Cornelius. Historiae.
Classification: LCC PA6705.H6 B1 2018 | DDC 937/.07–dc23 LC record available
at https://lccn.loc.gov/2017049946

ISBN: PB: 978-1-3500-1015-4
       ePDF: 978-1-3500-1018-5
       epub: 978-1-3500-1016-1

Typeset by RefineCatch Limited, Bungay, Suffolk

To find out more about our authors and books visit www.bloomsbury.com
and sign up for our newsletters.

Contents

Preface

The introduction and notes in this edition are designed to support students who are reading Tacitus' *Histories* I in preparation for OCR's AS and A-level Latin examinations in June 2019–June 2021.

The selection concerns the initial events of A D 69, the Year of the Four Emperors. The narrative is fast-paced, with rebellion and violence breaking out in the city of Rome, as the Praetorian Guard of the emperor Galba transfer their support to a controversial younger man, Otho. In his trademark prose Tacitus vividly portrays the elderly Galba's attempts to maintain order and discipline as power slips from his grasp, while Otho inspires the disorderly soldiers, keeping control only with difficulty over this volatile group of men.

The notes focus mainly on matters of language and aim to help those who have mastered the language requirements of Latin GCSE to decipher Tacitus' often elusive prose. Attention is devoted primarily to issues of syntax and grammar, and the authors take the view that without a real understanding of how the Latin is working, students will not be able to engage with and comment on the text. At the end of the book is a full vocabulary list for all the words contained in the prescribed sections, with words in OCR's Defined Vocabulary List for AS Level Latin flagged by means of an asterisk.

Particular features of Tacitus' style, and stylistic devices that are more difficult to spot, have also been noted in the commentary, but it has been a purposeful decision not to point out every instance of alliteration or repetition, for example, in the hope that students will make their own discoveries and develop their own ability to form views and opinions on the text. The commentary also provides help with names of people and places, specific historical events and technical terms, and this is supported by glossaries, maps and a timeline. We hope that with the help of this edition the keen student will gain an appreciation of what makes personal engagement with Tacitus and his style of historical narrative such a rewarding experience.

Ellen O'Gorman wrote the introduction, and Benedict Gravell the notes and vocabulary. We are particularly grateful to the very helpful comments made by Bloomsbury's anonymous reviewer on the first draft, as well as OCR for their input and amendments. Thanks also go to Alice Wright and the rest of her team at Bloomsbury for all their work and professionalism.

Ellen O'Gorman
Benedict Gravell
May 2017

Introduction

The scope of the *Histories*, and the importance of the military

In the preface to the *Histories* Book I, Tacitus outlines the subject matter of his work, emphasizing the violent and revolutionary events that will occur between the years AD 69 and 96: *opus aggredior opimum casibus, atrox proeliis, discors seditionibus, ipsa etiam pace saevum* (*Hist.* I.2.1); 'I embark upon a history replete with disaster, ferocious with battles, torn apart by revolts, and, even in peace, savage'. He goes on to list the many civil and foreign wars that occupied Rome at this time, as well as the great calamities of the period – how the citizens of Rome itself set fire to and destroyed their central temple, the Capitol* (all words with asterisks are explained in the Glossary of Technical Terms), at the end of 69, and how the eruption of Vesuvius ten years later obliterated the towns of Pompeii and Herculaneum – culminating with the reign of terror visited upon the senatorial class by the emperor Domitian, until his assassination in 96 (all dates in this Introduction are AD). This dramatic series of events made up Tacitus' first long historical narrative, which was probably 12 or 15 books long. Today, we have Books I–IV and a small part of Book V, and most of this narrative (Books I–III) is devoted to the civil war of 69: the 'year of four emperors'. What attracted Tacitus to this period of Roman history?

For Tacitus, the events of this year laid bare a fundamental truth about the power of emperors at Rome: that the senate may name the emperor, but it was the armies who made and sustained him as the first man in the city and the empire. Tacitus articulates this truth rather obliquely in the first chapter of our set text: *evulgato imperii arcano posse principem alibi quam Romae fieri* (*Hist.* I.4.2); 'When the secret of rule was made public knowledge: a princeps* (an emperor) can be made in some place other than at Rome'. By *alibi quam Romae* Tacitus meant the legionary camps stationed around the provinces of the empire, where soldiers gathered in their own political assemblies, and acclaimed their own legionary legates, or provincial governors, with the title *imperator*. In this year, four successive emperors were declared in some place other than the senate of Rome: **Galba**, governor in Spain, was backed by the single legion* of that province and raised a second legion with the financial support of neighbouring governors; **Otho** was declared emperor in the Praetorian Camp stationed on the outskirts of the city, and was also backed by some troops quartered in the city; **Vitellius**, as governor of Lower Germany, had the support of the legions in both Lower and Upper Germany (seven in total); and **Vespasian**, governor of Judaea and commander of the Jewish war, was declared emperor first in Alexandria, then in Judaea and Syria (eight legions in total), and subsequently received the backing of the six legions in Moesia and Pannonia (modern-day Austria). After the relatively smooth dynastic succession of the Julio-Claudian emperors (the dynasty started by Augustus, and ending with Nero), Romans must have been thrown into disarray by the incursion of so many armed rulers from the edges of their empire.

Rome was not allowed to forget this fundamental truth about military force. The last emperor of 69, Titus Flavius Vespasianus, or Vespasian, established a stable regime and ruled for ten more years. Each year, he celebrated his *dies imperii*, or anniversary of coming to rule, on 10 July – the day he had been declared emperor by the legions of Egypt – rather than on 4 January, the day six months later when the senate at Rome formally ratified his position. Vespasian was reminding the senate and people that his power base resided with the military, and was out of their control. On his death, he was succeeded first by his elder son, **Titus**, who survived his father by only two years, and then by his younger son, **Domitian** (81–96): both rulers were successful military commanders, and popular with the provincial legions and the Praetorian Guard*, the prestigious military force tasked with protection of the emperor in the city. When Domitian, hated by the senators if not by the soldiers, was assassinated in 96 by a small group of conspirators, and the senate named in his place an elderly senator named **Nerva**, the armies were not impressed. Six months into Nerva's reign, he was faced with a mutiny of the Praetorian Guard. Blockaded in the imperial residence on the Palatine*, Nerva was forced to make concessions to the Praetorians, and it brought home to him the truth that Rome had learned nearly 30 years earlier: the armies could both make and unmake an emperor. In the following weeks, Nerva announced that he was adopting an heir and successor – the experienced military commander M. Aelius Traianus, or **Trajan**, who was currently waging war in Pannonia. Nerva's choice appealed to the soldiers as well as to many in the senate, and stability was gradually restored.

Tacitus was suffect consul* (secondary consul) in the months after Trajan's adoption had been announced. He cannot have been the only Roman whose thoughts went back to the crisis of 69, when Galba began to lose the support of the armies in Germany, and, like Nerva, sought to increase confidence in his rule by adopting a successor, **Piso**. Unlike Nerva, Galba failed to appease the Praetorian Guard, who were won over to the support of the senator Otho. As news spread through the city of the soldiers' defection, Galba and his advisors blockaded themselves in the Palatine. When they finally emerged and mingled with the panic-stricken people of Rome, it was too late to regain control. On Otho's command, the soldiers charged into the Forum*, killing those in their path. Galba and his fellow-consul Titus Vinius were brutally murdered; the imperial heir, Piso, took shelter in the temple of Vesta, from which he was dragged out and killed. The surviving senators scrambled to the Praetorian Camp outside the city, swearing allegiance to their new emperor.

Galba's fate, then, seemed strikingly relevant to the new emperor Nerva, and Tacitus as senator and historian must have seen the importance of setting out Galba's history and its aftermath, so that he and his readers could fully understand the differences and similarities between past and present, take full advantage of the opportunities of their present situation, and remain aware of its dangers.

This is the historical context that illuminates Tacitus' emphasis, in the opening chapters of the narrative, on the state of mind among the soldiers. Over Chapters 4–5, he devotes two lines to the senate, half a line to the *equites**, and four lines to the people, plebs* and slaves (*Hist.* I.4.2). But the attitude of the *miles urbanus* is explored over fourteen lines, with the long, convoluted syntax reflecting the warring motivations of loyalty, greed, guilt, and distaste for the new emperor's strictness (*Hist.* I.5.1–2). The length of treatment signals the importance of the role played by soldiers in the historical events which will unfold: as Tacitus goes on to say, they are *ingens novis rebus materia* (*Hist.* I.6.2); 'the raw material for revolution'. By sketching out the different motivations, Tacitus presents us with a psychologically and historically complex portrait of the men who underpin the emperor's power. It is worth examining this significant passage in some detail.

The soldier's allegiance rests on **symbolic** and **material** supports. By declaring an oath of loyalty to the emperor every year, the army **symbolically** reasserts their relationship to the emperor, and this tradition is so embedded in the military that violating the oath of loyalty causes them unease. Hence Tacitus says the *miles urbanus* is *longo Caesarum sacramento imbutus* (*Hist.* I.5.1); 'steeped in the long-standing oath to the Caesars'. In Chapter 36, we see the attentiveness with which the rebel Praetorians administer a new oath, holding on to each individual soldier, and not releasing him until his allegiance to

Otho is assured (*Hist.* I.36.2). The many accounts of mutiny across the first three books of the *Histories* show us that breaking the oath of loyalty only occurs in situations of extreme violence and disorder, and that the men often experience continued unrest after they have switched allegiance. In this early chapter, Tacitus uses this idea to outline the Praetorian Guard's guilty conscience at having disregarded their oath to protect the emperor Nero. Here Tacitus alludes to a period of history that would be very well known to his readers. The Praetorian Prefect*, Nymphidius Sabinus, who was in charge of the Praetorian Guard, had persuaded his men to transfer their support to Galba by telling them that Nero had deserted them. Later Nymphidius, having received little encouragement from Galba, made the rash decision to declare himself emperor before Galba reached Rome. His own soldiers would not accept this declaration: they killed Nymphidius in the camp, and displayed his body outside for two days. Despite their prompt action, however, the soldiers continued to feel unease at their implication in Nero's downfall and Nymphidius' attempted coup. Hence Tacitus says *manebat plerisque militum conscientia* (*Hist.* I.5.2); 'A bad conscience continued to nag at many of the soldiers'.

But the army did not march on conscience alone. In addition to their military pay, and wealth acquired by looting in war, soldiers relied on occasional handouts from their rulers: the tradition of the **donative*** went back to the late Republic, and sealed the relationship between army and commander. Nymphidius was able to persuade the Praetorian Guard because he promised them that Galba would give each man 30,000 HS (ten times his annual salary); the legionary soldiers were expecting a donative of 5,000 HS (more than five times their annual salary): while a soldier's salary identified the soldier in terms of the work he did, the donative identified the soldier as the emperor's man. Consequently a soldier's ambition – his aspiration to improve his own financial status – could be more effectively achieved by participating in a military coup than by fighting in service of the state. In this paradoxical situation, Romans experienced their own soldiers as predators rather than protectors. Tacitus presents two dramatic scenes to illustrate this: first when the Praetorian Guard invaded the Forum to eliminate Galba (*Hist.* I.40.2); second, when the soldiers of Vitellius and Vespasian turned the streets of the city into a battleground, while the Romans cheered them on (*Hist.* III.85).

The promise of a donative was traditional, but the amount promised by Nymphidius was obscene, and almost certainly could not have been borne by the state after the reign of Nero, who had bankrupted Rome with his building projects and gifts to favourites. In any case, Galba had no intention of paying out any money. He may have been motivated by the poor state of the public finances (discussed with the senate in Chapter 20), but it also seems that he was well known to be tight-fisted with money. This is presented as a feature of Galba's old-fashioned sense of military discipline; Tacitus quotes his slogan *legi a se militum, non emi* (*Hist.* I.5.2); 'He was accustomed to choose his soldiers, not buy them'. Tacitus agrees with Galba up to a point: he too deplores the way that the prospect of financial reward leads soldiers to abandon loyalty, discipline, and patriotism, and his account of how Otho bought the favour of the Praetorians is conveyed in strong tones of moral disapproval (*Hist.* I.23–26). At the same time, Tacitus expresses exasperation at Galba's inflexible integrity, and leaves open the possibility that this moral rectitude is simple greed – *avaritia*. When Galba announced his choice of successor at the Praetorian Camp, he was received with little enthusiasm, and Tacitus identifies this moment as a missed opportunity to win over the soldiers with a little material reward: *constat potuisse conciliari animos quantulacumque parci senis liberalitate; nocuit antiquus rigor et nimia severitas, cui iam pares non sumus* (*Hist.* I.18.3); 'It is agreed by historians that Galba could have mollified the soldiers with even the tiniest little amount of generosity from a miserly old man; but his old-fashioned rigour and excessive strictness did him damage, since we are no longer able to come up to such standards'. In the drawn-out syllables of *quantulacumque* we can hear Tacitus' frustration: the army may be unreasonable in demanding a donative, but these are the times we (Tacitus and his readers) live in. If Galba had recognized this, perhaps a violent revolution could have been forestalled.

Galba's *severitas* has already been pointed out in Chapter 5 as a source of anxiety for the soldiers, and here Tacitus identifies a fundamental problem for the emperors in their interactions with the military: how can an emperor maintain **discipline** over soldiers who have become accustomed to being courted by their rulers? Galba's attempt to impose old-style Roman military discipline only alienated the soldiers, and once more Tacitus indicates that this is partly the fault of the soldiers – who had lost their hardiness under Nero's dissolute guidance – and partly the fault of Galba himself. Chapter 6 outlines very briefly an incident that marked Galba's arrival into the city as an ill-omened event. Soldiers attached to the Roman fleet presented demands to the new emperor as he approached the Mulvian Bridge. Galba's response to their mutiny was first to decimate the troops (killing one soldier for every ten in the group), and then to execute any known ringleaders who survived. As Tacitus points out, this was *ipsis etiam qui occiderant formidolosus* (*Hist.* I.6.2); 'A frightful occurrence, even for those who carried out the killing'. It is hardly surprising that, when Otho addressed the troops who hailed him as emperor, he declared that 'what others call crime, Galba calls correction, and he gives false names to his behaviour: "*severitas*" to his savagery, "frugality" to his greed, and "discipline" to his torture and insult of you' (*Hist.* I.37.4).

Otho effectively courted the soldiers away from Galba, but his experience for the rest of Book I and the first half of Book II demonstrates a different aspect of the problems emperors face in dealing with their power base. As Tacitus pointedly remarks in the aftermath of Galba's murder; 'Otho did not have the authority to

prevent the soldiers' crimes – he could only order them' (*Hist.* I.45.2).
This was not just a problem for the emperor, as the violent crimes of
the soldiers were visited on the citizens of Rome, and especially the
senatorial class. Near the end of the first book, the Praetorian Guard's
suspicion of the senate broke out in paranoid conviction that Otho
had been killed, and they burst into the palace, threatening the dinner-
guests of their emperor (*Hist.* I.80–82). This brought home to Otho
how volatile the relationship with the military had become: the
soldiers refused to accept any intermediary, or any chain of command,
demanding instead unmediated access to the ruler they had made.
Since the chain of command is essential to the structure of a large
military force, Otho's army became effectively non-functional, with
disastrous consequences when they marched north to meet the
legions of Vitellius coming down from Germany. As Tacitus observes,
the soldiers were suspicious of other, sometimes more experienced,
military commanders, and trusted only Otho (*Hist.* II.33); his absence
from the decisive Battle of Bedriacum weakened the confidence of his
army, resulting in their defeat by the Vitellian forces. The final act of
Otho's reign demonstrates beyond doubt the strength of the
relationship he had forged with his men, even as it illustrates how
unproductive that relationship became for their respective ambitions.
As Otho took his own life to prevent further bloodshed, the army
broke out in inconsolable lamentation and some individual soldiers
voluntarily followed their emperor in death.

The following two emperors each maintained a more mediated
relationship with their armies, and much of the blame for the atrocities
in North Italy and Rome for the rest of the year is laid on Vitellius'
commanders Valens and Caecina, and Vespasian's second in command
Antonius Primus. Vitellius is presented as too feeble, and Vespasian as
too far away, to have much effect on the soldiers, but Tacitus continues
to represent the military as a capricious and violent force, only
partially under the control of their generals.

We see this in the language Tacitus uses to describe how emotions and loyalties shift and spread across these large groups of armed men. As Otho went to work on the *studia militum* in Chapter 23, their change of sympathy is conveyed through metaphors of fire and disease: two destructive forces that cannot be fully checked or directed. The centurion of the Praetorian Guard, Maevius Pudens, 'added flames, so to speak, to the fire of the soldiers' minds' – *flagrantibus iam militum animis velut faces addiderat Maevius Pudens* (I.24.1). Thus his act is both inflammatory and profoundly irresponsible. The spread of mutiny to other legions stationed in the city is like an infectious disease transmitted across a close-knit community: *infecit ea tabes legionum quoque et auxiliorum motas iam mentes* (I.26.1); 'the pestilence also infected the already affected minds of the legions and auxiliaries'. Tacitus continues the medical metaphor, and the theme of irresponsible behaviour, by pointing out that the disease of mutiny had symptoms (*indicia*), which the Praetorian Prefect Laco could have recognized and acted against, were it not for his criminal ignorance and apathy. With these metaphors of disease and fire, therefore, Tacitus presents a compelling picture of how difficult it is to control an armed force in a time of civil disturbance.

Tacitus: politician, orator, historian

In 97 the new emperor Nerva was establishing his control over the state, the armies were appeased by the adoption of Trajan as imperial heir, and Tacitus had attained the most senior position in the senate – the rank of consul*. His political career up to that point had spanned the reigns of three emperors, and overlapped with the period of history he was about to write about in the *Histories*. As he tells us himself in the preface: *mihi Galba Otho Vitellius nec beneficio nec iniuria cogniti. dignitatem nostram a Vespasiano inchoatam, a Tito* *auctam, a Domitiano longius provectam non abnuerim* ... (I.1.3); 'Neither Galba, Otho or Vitellius paid any favourable or damaging attention to me. I would not deny that my senatorial status was begun by Vespasian, it was considerably increased by Titus, and promoted much further by Domitian ...'

If Tacitus was born around 56 or 58, as is generally supposed, it would have been highly unlikely that he would have come to the attention of the emperors in 69, when he would have been no more than 13 years old. As a young man in the last years of Vespasian' reign, Tacitus would have been the right age to become a decemvir*, a junior magistrate in court, which gave him senatorial status (what he calls his *dignitas*) and started him on his senatorial career. Tacitus' father was of equestrian status, not a senator, but his position as an imperial procurator*, in charge of financial administration in Gallica Belgica, was already a sign that the emperor had taken notice of this family, and was making use of their services. Nevertheless, Tacitus could not have taken it for granted that he would become a member of the senatorial class, still less such a successful one, so Vespasian's support in granting Tacitus his *dignitas* is remembered by the historian with gratitude as well as pride. Since he goes on to say that his status was increased under Titus, we can suppose that he may have been elected quaestor* during that emperor's short reign; certainly he would have been the right age (25) for the magistracy in 81. The quaestorship ensured Tacitus' entry into the senate, and we know from an inscription that he followed the usual career path by serving as a tribune of the plebs in the years intervening this office and the next traditional position on the career path, the praetorship. It was usual for young senators to reach the rank of praetor* at the age of about 30, and Tacitus himself confirms this in his later work, the *Annals*, by dating his magistracy to the year 88:

> *nam is [Domitianus] quoque edidit ludos saeculares, iisque intentius*
> *adfui sacerdotio quindecimvirali praeditus ac tunc praetor. quod non*

iactantia refero, sed quia collegia quindecimvirum antiquitus ea
cura, et magistratus potissimum exsequebantur (Annals XI.11.1)

For Domitian also put on the secular games, and I assisted
with particular attentiveness, having been honoured with the
quindecimviral priesthood [a college of priests overseeing religious
matters important to the city], and being praetor at the time. I do
not mention this in order to boast, but because from antiquity the
college of quindecimviri have had oversight of the secular games,
and it is especially the duty of the magistrates to carry them out.

The combination of the praetorship – the magistracy that qualifies
senators for senior posts – and a highly prestigious priesthood is
clearly what Tacitus means when he says, in the preface to the *Histories*,
that his career was considerably promoted under Domitian. It was
most likely Domitian, too, who placed Tacitus' name on the list to be
consul in 97, a position which was then confirmed by the new emperor
Nerva. The important point to note about Tacitus' career is how
smoothly it progressed; he achieved all the requisite magistracies at
the right age, or even a little earlier. When he reached the consulship
– the pinnacle of a Roman political career – he may have been only
39: a striking achievement for a man whose family was relatively new
to the senatorial class. There are several factors that could have
supported him in this successful career: he is at pains to emphasize
the favour of the three Flavian emperors, and it is very likely that
Tacitus earned this favour by his service in different posts between his
magistracies; it is now conjectured also that Tacitus may have had
useful senatorial links through his mother's family; what is certain is
that Tacitus' own considerable talents as an orator contributed to his
success.

Public speaking, whether in the law courts or the senate house, was
essential to anyone who wanted to further their career and status in
Rome. The ability to speak well enabled a man to influence political
decisions, protect his friends, and extend his own wealth and power.

Tacitus, it appears, was one of the best orators of his generation; Pliny the younger, his friend and colleague, refers to Tacitus as *eloquentissimus* (*Epistles* II.1.6) and adds that 'the outstanding feature of his style is his solemnity' (II.11.17) – and Pliny's judgement was based on his own extensive experience of oratory. He also records the anecdote, passed onto him by Tacitus himself, that Tacitus was asked by a Roman equestrian whether he was an Italian or a provincial. When Tacitus replied that the equestrian should know him from his literary activity, the man responded, 'Then, are you Tacitus or Pliny?' (*Epistles* IX.23). When Tacitus took up the consulship at the end of 97, therefore, he was well known for his excellence in oratory. Yet as the reign of Nerva ended and Trajan's began, and as Tacitus continued as a senior statesmen in Rome and abroad, he also turned to a new genre of writing: history.

The transition from politician and orator to historian was not as abrupt as it might initially seem; the majority of histories written in Rome were by men who had been politically active. Moreover, two of the shorter works that Tacitus produced before he started on the *Histories* were concerned as much with oratory as with the past: his biography of his father-in-law, **Agricola**, substituted for the funeral speech that Tacitus had been unable to deliver on Agricola's death in 93, when he was abroad as a provincial legate; the **Dialogus de Oratoribus**, a debate set in the reign of Vespasian, presents the great speakers of Tacitus' youth exploring the question of whether oratory has changed from the Republic to the Principate* (the period of imperial rule starting with Augustus). Although the debate is never finally settled, the concluding argument states emphatically that the opportunities for a speaker to exercise political influence are more restricted under the emperors. Many readers consider that Tacitus uses the *Dialogus* to express his disenchantment with the oratory he had practised throughout his adult career, and such an interpretation could be borne out by examining the speeches in *Histories* I. In the first half of the book, the set speeches of Galba (in the private space of the palace), Piso (on the steps of the palace), and Otho (in the praetorian camp) dramatize the diversion of politically significant speech away from the senate (which barely features in the first book). By juxtaposing these speeches with their effects on the audience (sometimes effects that the speakers did not intend), Tacitus the historian is able to deploy his rhetorical skills while suggesting to his readers that rhetorical skill has its limits in the new political landscape.

There was another reason why the writing of history might have seemed attractive to Tacitus at this stage in his career. As we have seen, his first short work, *Agricola*, is a eulogy of his father-in-law, published five years after his death. Agricola had a successful political career, most notably as governor of Britain from 77 to 84, but on his return to Rome he was no longer considered for prestigious posts. It seems that Agricola no longer enjoyed the imperial favour that still sustained his son-in-law. In 98, then, Tacitus recounted Agricola's life and achievements in order to restore a memory that he felt was at risk of being obliterated in the reign of Domitian. This is an important aspect of Tacitus' attitude to the past; he was not simply putting together and writing up 'what everybody knows', but was actively trying to retrieve knowledge of the past that had been distorted and suppressed in the interests of those in power. We see the same sense of urgency in his approach to the subject-matter of the *Histories*. Here the truth has been obscured or twisted out of recognition by the partisanship of writers, supporting or undermining specific emperors: *veritas pluribus modis infracta ... libidine assentandi aut rursus odio adversus dominantes. ita neutris cura posteritatis inter infensos vel obnoxios* (*Hist.* I.1.1); 'Truth was fractured in different ways ... by the desire for flattering agreement or conversely by hatred of those in power. So, between hostile and fawning historians, on neither side was there any care for the knowledge of posterity.'

The problem was particularly acute during the civil war, because each new emperor needed to represent himself as a legitimate ruler, and this often entailed blackening the character of his predecessor (from whom the new ruler had 'rescued' the state). We see Galba using the example of Nero as the tyrant from whom he has liberated Rome – throughout the set text Galba's key propaganda term *consensus* is invoked (sometimes ironically). Otho, by contrast, seeks to represent Galba as a ruler of excessive severity and cruelty, and he exploits the positive memory of Nero to bolster his own public image. Galba's memory was rehabilitated somewhat under Vitellius, as were both Galba's and Otho's under Vespasian, who was at pains primarily to discredit his opponent Vitellius. In the aftermath of the Flavian dynasty, Tacitus was faced with the task of picking through all these partisan accounts, and making an impartial judgement about the truth of the matter. We see this in the set reading, when he recounts the hostile and laudatory traditions about Galba's last moments (I.41.2), and he explicitly addresses the problem of partisan histories at the end of the second book, discussing the betrayal of Vitellius by two of his commanders:

> *scriptores temporum, qui potiente rerum Flavia domo monimenta belli huiusce composuerunt, curam pacis et amorem rei publicae, corruptas in adulationem causas, tradidere. nobis super insitam levitatem et prodito Galba vilem mox fidem aemulatione etiam invidiaque . . .*
>
> (*Hist.* II.101.1)

Contemporary historians, who wrote accounts of this war while the Flavian emperors were in power, claimed that these commanders were motivated by concern for peace, and love of their state, reasons which have been distorted in order to flatter. My opinion, however, is that, in addition to their characteristic fickleness and their loyalty which had already been cheapened by betraying Galba, these two men were motivated by rivalry and resentment . . .

Tacitus identifies *adulatio* – the historian's desire to flatter Vespasian and his heirs – as something that corrupts the historical record; this is the same problem he had identified in the preface as *libido assentandi* – the desire for flattering agreement. But Tacitus also benefitted from Vespasian's favour, so his refusal here to go along with the party line about those who abandoned Vitellius to join Vespasian is designed to demonstrate to his reader that he, at least, will remain uncorrupted. This is also how he reassures the reader in the preface, as he recounts his political career, in a passage examined above, at the beginning of this section. To this he adds: . . . *sed incorruptam fidem professis neque amore quisquam et sine odio dicendus est* (I.1.3); '. . . but no emperor should be spoken of with excessive affection or hatred by those of us who are committed to incorruptible truth'.

This is how Tacitus escapes the throng of hostile and fawning historians and proclaims his fidelity to truth. But does this mean that Tacitus is entirely unbiased? It's fair to say that there is no such thing as an unbiased historian, although some have a greater commitment to truth than others. It would have been interesting to see how Tacitus wrote about emperors who were still living and could react to his historical judgement. But he only makes a few cursory remarks about Nerva and Trajan, promising to write about them more fully in a later work. He introduces this promise immediately after his assertion that no emperor should be spoken of with excessive affection or hatred: *quod si vita suppeditet, principatum divi Nervae et imperium Traiani, uberiorem securioremque materiam, senectuti seposui, rara temporum felicitate ubi sentire quae velis et quae sentias dicere licet* (*Hist.* I.1.4); 'But, if a period of life is left for me after this, I have set aside for my old age the topic of the divine Nerva's principate and the rule of Trajan, that rare happiness of times when you are permitted to think you want, and say what you think'.

It is easy to dismiss this as the necessary flattery of the present ruler, but Tacitus is also making a subtle point about the relationship between the historian's commitment to truth, and the good ruler's commitment to a regime that encourages truth-telling. If we see Tacitus' *Histories* as an example of a historian striving to achieve an objective judgement of the past, Tacitus suggests that this is in part because he lives under an emperor who enables this sort of objective judgement.

Though Tacitus lived long under Trajan, and was probably still writing under Hadrian, he never went on to write that promised history of Nerva and Trajan; instead, his final and best-known work, the **Annals**, went back to the first dynasty of emperors, starting from the death of Augustus in 14, and working up to the deposition and death of Nero in 68. This narrative joined up with the *Histories* to form a continuous account of most of the first century. Some scholars suggest that Tacitus went back further in the past because he was reluctant to write about the present ruler, but it is also clear that the *Annals* provided Tacitus with the opportunity to explore further some of the themes that were so important to him in the earlier works. In particular, he was interested in how power had become concentrated in one person, the emperor, and what role that left for senators, men like him, in the Roman state. Tacitus clearly felt that to understand this, he needed to go back to the earliest emperors, and trace the development of their interaction with the senate up to the generation before his own political career began. His vivid account in the *Annals* of the family of Julio-Claudian emperors, and how their dynastic politics played out in the senate and across the empire, has captured the imagination of readers from the sixteenth century to the present day. Although the topic and atmosphere of the first half of *Histories* I seems quite different from the world of the *Annals*, the two works have more in common than it might seem at first glance. The *Annals* also begins with the new emperor, Tiberius, attempting to calm the mutinous legions that threaten to nominate a new ruler. Unlike the emperors of 69, he is successful in maintaining power, but this episode in *Annals* I clearly looks forward to the more disruptive events of *Histories* I. A recurrent theme throughout the *Annals* is the possibility of free speech under the emperors, and the narrative breaks off in

Book 16 at the suicide of a fiercely independent senator (Thrasea Paetus) in the reign of Nero. In the *Histories* we see the same issues facing the senators who survive the civil war and negotiate their relationship with the new emperor Vespasian: prominent in Book 4 of the *Histories* is the outspoken Helvidius Priscus, son-in-law of Thrasea Paetus. It is very likely that Tacitus knew the descendants of these men, and may even have been distantly related to them; certainly he would have recognized the issues they faced in their political lives, trying to avoid the displeasure of autocratic rulers while remaining true to what they believed was the right way to act.

The characters of *Histories* I

Otho and Piso: the rivals for succession

An important element of survival under autocratic rulers was to recognize the kind of man you were dealing with, and to understand the extent to which you could influence his action. Hence, the focus on character in historical and biographical accounts of emperors reflects its political significance for those living at the time. This is dramatized early in *Histories* I when Galba is confronted with the need to adopt a successor, and assesses the characters of the two main rivals for the position, **Otho** and **Piso**. As well as setting up an opposition that is explored further throughout the narrative leading up to Piso's death, this adoption scene is also notable for the way that Tacitus extends Galba's judgement of the two men into a more complex evaluation of character from different points of view. As elsewhere in his account, Tacitus creates our sense of the characters from a combination of **value judgements, behaviour, speech** and the **company** they keep. This last attribute is clearly at the forefront of Galba's mind when he rejects Otho as an heir: *credo et rei publicae curam subisse, frustra a Nerone translatae si apud Othonem relinqueretur* (I.13.2); 'I also believe that concern for the state impelled Galba's choice, as he thought that it would be pointless to have removed Rome from Nero's power, if it was then to be left in Otho's care'. Everyone in the narrative follows Galba's observation in considering Otho to be a second Nero (though not everyone thinks that this is a bad thing). Indeed, once Otho does become emperor, he has to field popular demands to take on the name of Nero (*Hist.* I.78.2). Once Tacitus has presented Galba's rejection of Otho on these grounds, he amplifies the emperor's judgement by presenting a narrative of Otho's early life, which continually raises the question of whether being a friend of Nero really makes a man similar to Nero:

> *namque Otho pueritiam incuriose, adulescentiam petulanter egerat, gratus Neroni aemulatione luxus. eoque Poppaeam Sabinam, principale scortum, ut apud conscium libidinum deposuerat, donec Octaviam uxorem amoliretur. mox suspectum in eadem Poppaea in provinciam Lusitaniam specie legationis seposuit. Otho comiter administrata provincia primus in partis transgressus nec segnis et, donec bellum fuit, inter praesentis splendidissimus, spem adoptionis statim conceptam acrius in dies rapiebat, faventibus plerisque militum, prona in eum aula Neronis ut similem.*

> (I.13.3–4)

For Otho spent his childhood carelessly, as a young man was rather wild, and was favoured by Nero because of a rivalry in luxurious living. Nero entrusted Poppaea Sabina, the imperial whore, to Otho as a confidant of his intrigues, until he could dispose of his wife Octavia: then, suspecting Otho of carrying on with Poppaea, he settled him in Lusitania on the pretext of a provincial command. Otho ran the province benignly, was the first to go over to Galba's cause, and was active and exceptionally distinguished among his supporters during the revolt; hence he had immediately fostered hopes of being adopted, and desired this more fiercely with every day: most of the soldiers were well disposed towards him, and the court of Nero inclined strongly towards him because he was like Nero.

Although this initially comes across as a rather damning portrait, embroiling Otho in the emperor's sexual intrigues, and associating him with luxury and misspent youth, there are some elements that provoke the reader's thought. Particularly, Otho's management of Lusitania is slightly unexpected; a man given up to wild living would likely use his position to get rich at the expense of the province, but the adverb *comiter* instead suggests that Otho attended to the well-being of those under his command. Similarly, his activity in Galba's revolt – *nec segnis et . . . splendidissimus* – suggests that he provided Galba with some of the money necessary to raise a second legion; this generosity is not what readers would usually associate with a character who practises *luxus* and *libido*. These minor dissonances at the outset will be amplified throughout the portrayal of Otho, so that the positive portrayal of him a book later, marching out of Rome in military garb to meet the forces of Vitellius, will remind the reader of this first appearance, and suggest that we scrutinize more carefully the way in which Romans judge this emperor: *nec illi segne aut corruptum luxu iter, sed lorica ferrea usus est et ante signa pedes ire, horridus, incomptus famaeque dissimilis* (II.11.3); 'Otho's march was not idle or disgraced by luxury, but he wore an iron breastplate and went on foot, leading the standards, unshaven, scruffy, and quite different from his reputation'. The verbal echoes, especially at the end, between *Neronis similem* and *famae dissimilis*, prepare us for more unexpected elements to Otho's character.

This lengthy introduction of Otho in book I interrupts the adoption scene, to which we return with Galba's positive choice of Piso, who is presented almost immediately as a man *prospera fama* (I.14.1), 'of good reputation'. Indeed, he seems the polar opposite of Otho, having earned not the favour but the displeasure of Nero (by whom he was exiled). Here Tacitus presents us first with the narrative point of view on Piso's character, and only turns in the final two words to Galba's judgement of his new heir:

Piso M. Crasso et Scribonia genitus, nobilis utrimque, vultu habituque
moris antiqui et aestimatione recta severus, deterius interpretantibus
tristior habebatur: ea pars morum eius quo suspectior sollicitis
adoptanti placebat

(I.14.2)

Piso was the son of M. Crassus and of Scribonia, a nobleman on
both sides of his family, with old-fashioned manners in his
expression and bearing, and regarded correctly by some as severe,
but to those who put a worse construction on it he was considered
rather bad-tempered: that aspect of his behaviour, which was
suspected by those who were anxious, was pleasing to the man
about to adopt him.

Galba's choice – a man completely unlike Otho – also happens to
be a man very like Galba himself, who is hampered in his relations
with the army, as we have seen, by *antiquus rigor et nimia severitas*
(I.18.3). How reliable is Galba's judgement, or that of the *solliciti* who
are worried about an heir perhaps too much like the inflexible and
miserly emperor? Tacitus, however, throws his authorial weight
behind the more positive view of Piso, distinguishing between right
(*recta*) and worse (*deterius*) ways of interpreting behaviour. But, as
with the sketch of Otho, Tacitus has warned the reader that the
judgements of others are both illuminating and misleading for our
assessment of character.

All of this takes place before either Piso or Otho have spoken or acted
within the narrative; once they begin to do so, the contrast that has been
initially set up between them intensifies. Piso is initially presented as an
impassive, indeed almost unreadable figure: his 'expression and bearing',
already remarked upon in the original sketch, undergoes no change; his
limited speech is mentioned but not reported by Tacitus, either at the
palace (I.17.1) or when the adoption is announced in senate (I.19.1).
Tacitus concludes Piso's inauguration as Caesar with the ominous
statement *nec aliud sequenti quadriduo, quod medium inter adoptionem*

et caedem fuit, dictum a Pisone in publico factumve (I.19.1); 'In the
following four days which intervened between his adoption and his
murder, nothing was done or said by Piso in public'. By contrast, Otho's
furious response to the adoption emerges as energetic, focused activity,
and with a private speech in indirect discourse that further deepens the
complexities of his character, encompassing his decadent lifestyle and
his unexpected courage. If Piso is opaque to the reader, Otho is laid bare
in what amounts to a soliloquy. This begins unpromisingly with the
word *fingebat* – although this can mean 'to conceive or review' ideas, it is
difficult not to think that Otho is partly conjuring up fears in order to
justify acting on his desires: *fingebat et metum quo magis concupisceret*
(I.21.1); 'He conjured up fear to increase his aspirations'. Otho reminds
us of the danger he faced when Nero suspected him of adultery with
Poppaea, and turns this now into a general truth that is still relevant
under Galba: *suspectum semper invisumque dominantibus qui proximus
destinaretur* (I.21.1); 'The one who is pointed out as next in succession
is always suspected and hated by those in power'. In this way Otho
proceeds to argue for swift and decisive action, always combining
particular observations about the situation he finds himself in with
universalizing statements about power, opportunity, and finally virtue.
His final reflections, therefore, are quite incongruent when we look at the
beginning of this chapter, where Tacitus' comments emphasize the
dissolute side of Otho's character; by contrast, the soliloquy ends on a
note that looks forward to the courageous actions that will redeem his
reputation for posterity:

> *Othonem, cui compositis rebus nulla spes, omne in turbido consilium,
> multa simul extimulabant, luxuria etiam principi onerosa, inopia vix
> privato toleranda, in Galbam ira, in Pisonem invidia ... mortem
> omnibus ex natura aequalem oblivione apud posteros vel gloria
> distingui; ac si nocentem innocentemque idem exitus maneat,
> acrioris viri esse merito perire.*

> (I.21.1–2)

As for Otho, who had no hope in a settled state, whose every plan
required disturbance, he was spurred all at once by many motivations:
a luxurious lifestyle that would wear out a prince, debt hardly to be
born even by a private citizen . . . [he considered that] death, common
to all by nature, was differentiated by the oblivion or glory one
enjoyed in posterity; and if the same outcome awaited guilty and
innocent alike, it was the mark of a spirited man to die with merit.

Thus Tacitus embeds into his early characterization of Otho the
striking contrast, which intrigued all writers of the period, between
his dishonourable life and his admirable death. In the first part
of *Histories* I we see much more of the dishonourable – when he
abandons his dignity to curry favour with the soldiers (*serviliter pro
dominatione*, 1.36.3), for instance, or as he gazes with insatiable
pleasure on the decapitated head of his rival Piso (I.44.1) – but Tacitus
expects us never to lose sight of the dual nature of this unusual man.
After Otho's suicide, conducted with exemplary firmness, Tacitus
sums up his life as follows: *duobus facinoribus, altero flagitiosissimo,
altero egregio, tantundem apud posteros meruit bonae famae quantum
malae* (II.50.1); 'By two notable deeds, one the most disgraceful, the
other excellent, he earned in posterity as much good reputation as
bad'. Otho himself, in the closing words of his soliloquy, anticipates
this summary, as the repetition of *merito–meruit* makes clear.

Beside the flamboyant figure of Otho, actively forging relationships
with the Praetorian Guard to secure a military coup, the enigmatic
Piso seems to make little impression, beyond the gruesome details of
his murder and mutilation. He is, however, given a chance to contribute
to the series of speeches which punctuate the first half of *Histories* I,
and which position him as of equivalent importance to Galba (who
delivers a formal speech of adoption in Chapters 15–16) and Otho
(who harangues the soldiers in Chapters 37–38, and again in
Chapters 83–84). These speeches not only provide a further dimension
to the characters of the speakers; they also show us each speaker

attempting to initiate change in their world, impelling their listeners to some form of action. As we've already seen, Tacitus the orator was fully aware that persuasive speech was the primary mode of political action, and he invites his reader to evaluate characters' speeches for their truthfulness, consistency, and efficacy. Piso's speech, delivered to the cohort of the Praetorian Guard on guard duty at the palace, is often seen as an example of ineffective speech, a miniaturized and weaker version of Otho's address to the great mass of soldiers at the Praetorian Camp. But it is useful instead to consider how Piso attempts, under difficult circumstances, to forge a relationship with the military (with whom he has had no prior contact), create a public persona for himself, and align himself with the persona of his adoptive father. Thus he opens his speech by addressing the cohort as *commilitones*, a term used by both Galba (I.35.2) and Otho (I.37.1) with greater justification. But Piso's intention is to offer a shared sense of purpose between himself and the soldiers, building on Galba's attempt to win their favour by announcing the adoption first in the Praetorian Camp. So here Piso introduces himself as an adopted Caesar, but points out that the consequences of this adoption are entirely up to the soldiers: '*quo domus nostrae aut rei publicae fato in vestra manu positum est*' (I.29.2); 'It lies in your hands to determine what fate my adoption entails, for our family and for the state'.

Because of Piso's exile under Nero, he had had no opportunity to develop a political career through the successive magistracies and provincial posts that we have seen Tacitus himself holding. Instead, Piso constructs his authority in this speech on three bases: his experience of misfortune in exile; his care for the state; and his commitment to virtue. The experience of exile enables Piso to face his uncertain future with courage, and to emphasize that he speaks of that uncertainty not out of self-interest, but with a regard for the safety of the community as a whole. He underlines this point by switching from first person singular to plural forms, uniting himself with his audience in shared concern for the *res publica*: '*non quia meo nomine tristiorem casum paveam . . . patris et senatus et ipsius imperii vicem doleo, si nobis aut perire hodie necesse est aut, quod aeque apud bonos miserum est, occidere*' (I.29.2); 'It is not because I am afraid on my account at a more unfavourable outcome . . . I grieve for the fate of my father, the senate, and the empire itself, if we are required today to die, or, what is just as wretched a fate for good men, to kill'. Piso presents his virtue to the soldiers through a clever *praeteritio**, which also introduces his invective of Otho – the most negative portrayal of Otho in the text as a whole: '*neque enim relatu virtutum in comparatione Othonis opus est. vitia, quibus solis gloriatur, evertere imperium . . .*' (I.30.1); 'There is no need for me to tell you about my virtues in order to compete with Otho. His vices, which are all he has to boast of, have already ruined the empire . . .' In the ensuing list of Otho's immorality, the audience is expected to discern Piso's implicit good qualities: he is, we should presume, suitably manly, where Otho is effeminate; he displays *modestia* where Otho manifests *luxuria*; he has one respectable marriage, while Otho plots adulterous affairs. Above all, Piso continues to emphasize the consequences for Rome of such immoralities. Having begun his description of Otho with the claim that he 'ruined the empire' as Nero's friend, he concludes with the generalized truth '*nemo enim umquam imperium flagitio quaesitum bonis artibus exercuit*' (I.30.1); 'Nobody has ever run the empire with good behaviour, having acquired it with shameful acts'.

Finally, Piso aligns himself with Galba's self-representation, most notably when he echoes one of the emperor's most repeated slogans: '*Galbam consensus generis humani, me Galba consentientibus vobis Caesarem dixit*' (I.30.2); 'The consensus of the whole human race declared Galba emperor, and Galba declared me Caesar by your consent'. He thus echoes the earlier adoption speech, where Galba refers to himself as '*deorum hominumque consensu ad imperium vocatum*' (I.15.1); 'Called to rule by the consensus of gods and men'.

His commitment to virtue and to the state can also be seen as chiming in with the emperor's display of traditionalism and severity, and reinforces the way Piso was introduced in the narrative as a man very similar to his newly adopted father. But the danger of Piso's alignment with Galba is evident in the conclusion to the speech, when he remarks that the reward for loyalty is the same as for betrayal: *'proinde a nobis donativum ob fidem quam ab aliis pro facinore accipietis'* (I.30.2); 'In the end, you will receive a donative from us for your fidelity, as great as what you would receive from others for crime'. The obvious objection to this is that the much-spoken-of donative is never forthcoming – indeed, Galba did not even mention it in his speech to the Praetorians (I.18.2–3). Piso thus leaves himself open to the counter-charge that will be made in Otho's speech a few chapters later: '. . . *donativo quod vobis numquam datur et cotidie exprobratur*' (I.37.5); '. . . the donative which is never given to you, but is objected to every day'.

Piso was introduced to the narrative as a young man with *prospera fama* (I.14.1), 'a favourable reputation'; *prosperus* indicates hope for the future, but Tacitus very soon foreshadows his end, pointing to the *quadriduo, quod medium inter adoptionem et caedem fuit.* (I.19.1); 'The four days which intervened between his adoption and his slaughter'. In Piso's brief obituary, the moment where the man can be summed up once and for all, Tacitus returns to this idea that Piso's character had no bearing on the circumstances of his life, calling him a *quadriduo Caesar*, a 'four-day Caesar', and remarking that he lived *fama meliore quam fortuna* (I.48.1), 'with better reputation than fate'. In this Piso serves the greatest contrast with Otho, who manages to make his death the ultimate mark of his character.

Galba and his advisors

Piso appears in the narrative to be a rather isolated figure: he is friends with the Praetorian Prefect Cornelius Laco (I.14.2), though we never see them interact; he might be hostile to the consul Titus Vinius (I.34.1); he has a wife and brother, who are only mentioned when they retrieve Piso's body for burial (I.47.2: the wife, Verania, was still alive in Tacitus' day). Otho, on the other hand, is surrounded by advisors, but all of a lower or even disreputable class: his intimate freedmen and slaves, and, most damningly, astrologers (I.22). The company a man keeps is an indicator of his character, and can even exaggerate certain aspects of his behaviour. This is particularly the case with the emperor and his advisors, and a major concern of the historian is to gauge the extent of the advisor's influence.

Galba's character, as we've seen, is primarily old-fashioned, strict and frugal, but he is also surprisingly indecisive and susceptible to manipulation. Hence the characters of his main advisors are introduced early in the narrative, to alert the reader to the possibility that they have as much bearing as the emperor on the events that are to unfold. The way in which Tacitus chooses to introduce these two individuals is also significant; unlike the multi-layered presentation of Otho and Piso – and of Galba himself – from the perspective of other characters in the narrative, the opening judgement of Titus Vinius and Cornelius Laco is made in the narrator's own voice: *invalidum senem Titus Vinius et Cornelius Laco, alter deterrimus mortalium alter ignavissimus, odio flagitiorum oneratum contemptu inertiae destruebant* (I.6.1); 'Titus Vinius and Cornelius Laco, one the worst of mortals, the other the most cowardly, having already burdened the weak old man with hatred of Vinius' crimes, were about to bring him to destruction by contempt for Laco's passivity'. This damning summary distributes blame equally among all three individuals. The word order draws our attention to the weakness of Galba (whose passivity is reflected by his role in the sentence as direct object). This places his old age in a new context, after the preceding comments about the soldiers' attitude to his severity. Galba is, after all, the man who chose **Titus Vinius** to be consul alongside him in this first year of his reign, and elevated **Cornelius Laco** to one of the highest equestrian positions in the empire – Prefect of the Praetorian Guard. Tacitus thus implicitly places Galba's judgement of these men alongside his own, which is conveyed succinctly with the paired superlatives *deterrimus . . . ignavissimus*. Vinius and Laco are thereby introduced, and continue to act throughout the narrative, as a contrasting pair, representing two different ways of being the worst kind of man to advise an emperor.

The difference between Vinius' active vice – his *flagitia* – and Laco's *inertia* can be seen in the role each man plays as Otho gains control of the military: it is suspected that Vinius collaborates with Otho and intends to betray Galba, while Laco is simply too incompetent to notice that the soldiers under his command are about to switch their loyalties. Again, Tacitus underscores this difference in the way that he conveys these ideas to the reader. Laco's more straightforward moral failings continue to be pointed out in the narrator's voice, as when he remarks that Laco had in fact received warnings of the emerging coup, but had ignored them, *ignarus militarium animorum consiliique quamvis egregii, quod non ipse adferret, inimicus et adversus peritos pervicax* (I.26.2); 'Being completely ignorant of the state of mind of the soldiers, and hostile to any plan, however good, which he had not himself proposed – indeed, especially stubborn in opposition to those who knew better'. Laco being *ignarus* echoes his earlier introduction as *ignavus*, and the deadly combination of stupidity, obstinacy, and authoritative command makes him an obstacle to the emperor's success or survival.

Vinius, being a much more slippery character, is portrayed more allusively by Tacitus, who never really confirms or denies the rumours that he might be working for Otho. He certainly supports Otho's adoption, and his interest in doing so is attributed by rumour to ambition (I.13.2); that same ambition could prompt his continued support when Otho turned to seizing power by force. But the suspicions about Vinius are mostly conveyed through Laco's hostility to him in the advisory sessions after Otho has taken control of the

Praetorian Camp. In the first of these sessions, Laco advises Galba that it would be unwise to shelter in the Palace, and more honourable to take the initiative in meeting this danger (advice, incidentally, rather at odds with Laco's supposed *inertia*). When Vinius opposes this view, Laco verbally attacks the consul, egged on by Galba's favourite freedman Icelus (I.33.2). Why is the dispute so violent? This may be an illustration of Laco's obstinacy, but it may also point up his awareness of Vinius' villainy; an hour or so later, he is quietly canvassing the rest of the imperial council about killing Vinius. Here too, Tacitus avoids stating Laco's reasons directly, instead presenting the reader with alternative motivations: *sive ut poena eius animos militum mulceret, seu conscium Othonis credebat, ad postremum vel odio* (I.39.2); 'Whether he thought the punishment of Vinius would mollify the soldiers, or he suspected Vinius to be collaborating with Otho, or in the end just because he hated him'. Because Laco himself is such a discredited figure, we never know how much weight to give his suspicions of Vinius.

In the same way Tacitus both offers and withholds confirmation of Vinius' treachery in his account of the consul's death, and the obituary. Roman readers were fascinated by the last words of historical figures, which were supposed to sum up an individual's life and character. Tacitus thus concentrates on establishing what exactly both Galba and Vinius said when they met their violent ends, and comes up with quite different accounts. (This is another moment where Tacitus confronts the divergent traditions of partisan histories in the civil war, an issue we saw in the previous section.) Vinius' last words may help us to establish whether he really did betray his emperor: *de quo et ipso ambigitur consumpseritne vocem eius instans metus, an proclamaverit non esse ab Othone mandatum ut occideretur* (I.42.1); 'There is some doubt about Vinius too, whether fear pressing on him took away his voice altogether, or whether he shouted that Otho had not commanded his killing'. The problem with the latter version, Tacitus goes on to say, is that even if Vinius said these words we cannot rule out that he was lying in order to stall the executioners. But if he was collaborating – and Tacitus here repeats the damning word *conscius* from Laco's suspicions – it would be plausible, given Vinius' life and reputation: *huc potius eius vita famaque inclinat*. That is the nearest Tacitus comes to confirming the damning rumour, which he does not address in Vinius' obituary. There, instead, he provides a summary of the consul's character that concentrates on his energy: *audax, callidus, promptus et, prout animum intendisset, pravus aut industrius, eadem vi* (I.48.4); 'Daring, clever, quick and, wherever he directed his mind, degenerate or diligent, with the same active force'.

As we have already seen, the emperor Galba's character is first portrayed through the complex psychological portrait of the soldiers' state of mind, where Galba appears as a cause of anxiety and resentment. This is then immediately juxtaposed with his dangerous dependence on advisors such as Vinius and Laco. Galba's later judgement of Otho and Piso provides further perspective on the mixture of integrity, inflexibility, and gullibility in his character. While his speech of advice to his new heir contains much good sense, particularly about the need for a ruler to establish his own moral standards for ruling, the surrounding narrative suggests that Galba is not able to act on his own advice. The introductions to the scenes of debate in the imperial council are telling in this regard. The adoption debate begins *potentia principatus divisa in Titum Vinium consulem Cornelium Laconem praetorii praefectum* (I.13.1); 'The power of the principate was divided between the consul Vinius and the prefect Laco'. The absence of Galba, and the emphasis on division, undermines Galba's own sense of himself as the guardian of the state by universal agreement: *'me deorum hominumque consensu ad imperium vocatum'* (I.15.1); 'Myself, called to rule by the consensus of gods and men'. The next debate, over how to respond to the threat of Otho, begins: *interim Galbam duae sententiae distinebat* (I.32.2); 'Meanwhile, two opinions held Galba in suspense'. Here, *distinebat* conveys the idea of division again, but also of hindering the emperor – precisely the opposite of what imperial advice should convey. Again, as at I.6.1, quoted above, Galba's position as direct object in the sentence reflects how he is at the mercy of external forces, the *sententiae* of others.

The extent to which Galba is almost entirely dependent on what others say and do is given visual form when he dons armour and leaves the palace: *inopia veri et consensu errantium victus sumpto thorace Galba irruenti turbae neque aetate neque corpore resistens sella levaretur* (I.35.1); 'Overcome by the lack of true information and by ill-advised agreement, Galba put on his breastplate and, unable to stand up against the rushing crowd because of his old age and physical frailty, he was lifted up into a portable chair'. Many have observed the pathos of the old man putting on his warrior's garb, where Tacitus draws on some of the features of Vergil's Priam in Book I of *Aeneid*. What is significant here is that Galba is *victus* before he even sets out to battle, defeated by self-interested and ignorant advisors more than by his own bodily weakness. His precarious seat in the *sella* becomes symbolic of his failing grasp on power, as first he is tossed from side to side by the crowd of his own subjects (I.40.1), and finally tumbled to the ground as his carriers succumb to fear for their own safety (I.41.2). The visual image here reinforces the idea of the *invalidus senex*, as he was so emphatically named in Tacitus' introduction of Vinius and Laco (I.6.1).

Yet Galba's other marked characteristic, *severitas*, does not desert him; Tacitus makes sure to juxtapose the emperor's physical weakness with his continued strictness, by including a verbal exchange with one soldier, which foreshadows his final words to his assassins. As Galba is led off in his *sella*, he meets a *speculator*, Julius Atticus, who displays the same self-interest and disregard for truth as everyone else. Claiming to have killed Otho, he clearly hopes to receive a reward from the emperor, but instead he is reminded of the emperor's old-fashioned regard for military discipline: *et Galba 'commilito',* *inquit, 'quis iussit?' insigni animo ad coercendam militarem licentiam,* *minantibus intrepidus, adversus blandientes incorruptus.* (I.35.2); 'And Galba replied, "Comrade, who gave you such an order?" with his characteristic spirit in suppressing soldiers' lack of control, unintimidated by threats, uncorrupted in the face of flattery'. This is a striking contrast with the immediately preceding image of the emperor defeated by the speech of those around him. The same contrast is evident as Tacitus attempts to weigh up the different historical traditions about the emperor's last words (I.41.2). Did he plead for his life, and offer to pay the long-awaited donative? Or did he, as more sources attest, face up to his attackers and tell them to 'go ahead and kill him, if they thought that was what Rome needed'? In the earlier story of Julius Atticus, Tacitus has already told us what he thinks – Galba is by character *minantibus intrepidus* – so here at the end Tacitus makes no attempt to reconcile the divergent histories, leaving it up to the reader to make the final judgement. Instead, he presents the most chilling conclusion to the scene: *non interfuit* *occidentium quid diceret* (I.41.2); 'It made no difference to the killers what the emperor said'.

Tacitus' obituary of Galba is rightly one of the greatest character sketches of antiquity. It is the third successive obituary, which Tacitus places after the bodies of Piso, Vinius, and Galba have been recovered by their relatives, and it is clearly suggestive of the funeral oration that would normally have been delivered for a Roman aristocrat, commander, and consul, such as Galba had been. But it is measured rather than laudatory, drawing attention to how the emperor was *magis extra vitia quam cum virtutibus* (I.49.2); 'Free of vice rather than endowed with virtue'. Once more Tacitus shows us how the judgement of other characters is an integral feature of our understanding of Galba, when he points to how the emperor's nobility of birth, and the crisis of the civil war, led to people misinterpreting his lack of initiative (*segnitia*) as wisdom (*sapientia*) – the alliteration of the words points up the ease with which such misinterpretation can occur. The judgement of character is a difficult business, and Tacitus points this up with his memorable conclusion to the obituary: *maior privato visus dum privatus fuit, et omnium consensu capax imperii nisi imperasset* (I.49.4); 'Galba seemed to be more than just a private citizen – when he was a private citizen. By universal consensus he was capable of rule – if only he had not ruled'. *Consensus*, a term used by both Galba and Piso to promote confidence in their new dynasty, is here deployed to show how Galba did not live up to the expectations engendered by his own early life.

The style of Tacitus

History-writing was the highest form of prose literature in antiquity, and historians were expected to communicate their vision of the past through an impressive style of writing. Hence Tacitus followed his predecessors in cultivating formality and grandeur, but he also sought to create a distinctive literary voice. To this end, first he drew on the style of one of his most distinguished predecessors, C. Sallustius Crispus or **Sallust** (86–35 BC), and second he developed this style further in relation to the rhetorical taste of his late-first-century AD audience.

Sallust's historical works covered Roman history during 133–62 BC, and were concerned above all with the decline in Roman morality, and the consequences of this for the political health of the state. He communicated these concerns in writing that rebelled against the clarity and balance of what we now call 'classical Latin' (the prose style of Caesar and Cicero). Instead, Sallust cultivated an intense, disjointed style, choosing archaic words and abbreviating clauses and phrases to the point of obscurity. Tacitus aims at similar effects, probably because he was attracted as much to Sallust's view of history as to his literary manner. The dense abbreviated style also suited a writer of Tacitus' time, when literature was increasingly prized for innovative techniques, brilliance, and paradox. The trademark of first-century A D Latin was the **sententia*** or epigram: a punchy closing phrase in which extreme opposites were brought together with maximum economy of expression. Sallustian style lent itself well to this rhetorical feature, and there are several examples throughout *Histories* I. We have just seen how Tacitus ends his obituary of Galba with the *sententia, capax imperii nisi imperasset,* which uses repetition of related words (*imperium–imperare*) to point up a paradox about Galba's capacity to rule. The syncopated final word (*imperasset* for *imperavisset*) abbreviates and intensifies the expression. In similar vein, Tacitus frequently chooses the archaic and poetic abbreviation of third person plural perfect indicatives (*fuere* for *fuerunt*, 7.1; *anteposuere* for *anteposuerunt*, 28.1 – there are other examples in Chapters 30–43).

Another feature that can be identified is **variatio*** – the tendency to avoid paired or balanced constructions. We see this at a basic level in Tacitus' avoidance of constructions such as *alii . . . alii* (some people . . . other people): instead, we find *alios . . . quosdam* (I.23.1) or *alii . . . plerique* (I.27.2). It is also important to be alert to how Tacitus changes syntax in phrases that we would expect to be balanced: an early instance of this is the conclusion to Chapter 6, *ut non in unum aliquem prono favore ita audenti parata.* The *ut . . . ita* construction creates parallel phrases, but the syntax within them resists all parallels – *prono favore*, an ablative of description, is balanced by the nominative perfect participle *parata*, while the prepositional phrase *in unum aliquem* is supposed to match the dative present participle *audenti*. The broader uses of *variatio* often highlight moments where a choice has to be made between different interpretations of the events, so the imbalance of phrases makes an important point about how historical circumstances and meanings can hardly ever be placed in parallel. A useful example of this is the assessment of Galba's reasons for not investigating the killing of Fonteius Capito, where the first reason is given as a causal ablative, and the second as a negative purpose clause: *mobilitate ingenii, an ne altius scrutaretur* (I.7.2). Tacitus may seem to throw his weight behind the second reason, placing it more emphatically and articulating it more fully, but it might equally be the case that neither reason rules out the other.

In order to gain a fuller understanding of how Tacitus deploys Sallustian techniques of **brevitas*** and **disjointed structure**, it is useful to look more closely at how different features are used in a single passage of text, such as Chapter 22.1.

> *non erat Othonis mollis et corpori similis animus.* / [1] *et intimi libertorum servorumque,* / [2] *corruptius quam in privata domo habiti,* / *aulam Neronis et* [5] *luxus, adulteria, matrimonia ceterasque regnorum libidines* / *avido talium, si auderet,* [6] *ut sua ostentantes,* / [4] *quiescenti ut aliena exprobrabant,* / [7] *urgentibus etiam mathematicis,* / *dum novos motus et clarum Othoni annum observatione siderum adfirmant,* / [3] *genus hominum potentibus infidum, sperantibus fallax,* / [8] *quod in civitate nostra et vetabitur semper et retinebitur.*

Otho's mind was not soft, like his body. / And the most intimate of his slaves and freedmen, / who were maintained more decadently than in an ordinary citizen's household, / pointed out to him the court of Nero, and the luxuries, adulteries, marriages and other pleasures of kingly life, / (and he was greedy for such things): they pointed these out as his for taking, if he dared, / they reproached him when he seemed impassive, saying that these things would belong to another. / Meanwhile the astronomers were egging him on, / as they assured him that from the observation of the stars there were new movements afoot, and a bright year for Otho. / (Astronomers are a race of men faithless to the powerful, and deceitful to those who hope for power, / a race which will always be exiled from our state, and always be kept within it.)

In the long and convoluted second sentence [1], Tacitus uses **participle phrases** or **noun clauses** in apposition to describe Otho's various advisors or their actions; these are briefer and more intense than relative clauses: [2] *intimi ... corruptius quam in privata domo habiti* and [3] *mathematicis ... genus hominum potentibus infidum sperantibus fallax.* In the same way, Tacitus often uses a single **participle** instead of a temporal or relative clause, as he does here to show Otho's servants reproaching him when he does not act: [4] *quiescenti ... exprobrabant.* There are many examples of this vivid participle in the narrative, such as *sermones ... increpantium* (I.5.2) or *rumore ... computantium* (I.22.2). Tacitus increases the brevity and speed of the servants' exhortations with **asyndeton***, which is then varied by the introduction of one conjunction: [5] *luxus adulteria matrimonia ceterasque regnorum libidines.* Here it lends urgency to their pleas, as it does in the following chapter when Otho assiduously courts the soldiers: *in itinere in agmine in stationibus* (I.23.1). Further imbalance is created as Tacitus presents two actions of the servants in parallel, but changing between participle and finite verb so as to throw weight on the second action – [6] *ut sua ostentates ... ut aliena exprobrabant.* This sentence also provides an illustration of Tacitus' use of **appendix*** – a tendency to append subordinate clauses that overwhelm and displace the content of the main clause; here the **ablative absolute** that introduces [7] *urgentibus etiam mathematicis* shifts the reader's attention away from the servants in Otho's household towards these more glamorous hangers-on. Indeed, it could be said that the subordinate clauses throughout this sentence hold the most significant material. And, of course, the sentence concludes with a ***sententia*** about astrologers: [8] *genus ... quod in civitate nostra et vetabitur semper et retinebitur.* The paradox contained in the paired actions *vetabitur ... retinebitur* is pointed up by the similarity of endings (**homoioteleuton***), and intensified by *semper.* The jingle of *bitur ... bitur* is amplified by *et ... et*, which not only reinforces *semper,* but picks up on the homophony at the start of each verb: *et vet* . . . *et ret* . . .

This chapter also illustrates some aspects of Tacitus' **word choice**. He is attracted to words formed from -*mentum* (as later in this chapter with his reference to astrologers as *pessimum principalis matrimonii instrumentum* – compare I.20.1) and makes striking use of nouns in -*tor* (later in this chapter, Ptolemaeus is *sceleris instinctor*). Elsewhere there are several instances of Tacitus' inclination to use **abstract** instead of common nouns as subjects of verbs: *circumsteterat . . . publica exspectatio* instead of *circumsteterant populi exspectantes* (I.17.2); *patrum favor aderat* instead of *patres favore aderant* (I.19.1). Since the *Histories* was Tacitus' first full-length historical work, he had not yet developed the very distinctive style of the later books of the *Annals,* and this is evident in some of his word choices: he was already showing a preference for *cupido* rather than *cupiditas,* but we find him still using both forms in the *Histories* (*cupiditates,* I.12.2; *cupidine,* I.22.3), and his later marked preference for abstract nouns in -*tudo* rather than -*itas* (another rejection of classical norms) is not yet so obvious. Tacitus' style represents a challenge to the reader, who is expected to think about the relationship between all the parts of his sentences, and to ponder the meaning that is concealed there. It is very difficult to reproduce Tacitean style in English, and it is generally better to start by aiming for clarity in translation, even if that runs counter to Tacitus' overall effect; an example of this can be seen in the way the translation above approaches the long, impressionistic sentence of 22.1. Engaging with the Latin of this text has its rewards, as you will be drawn ever deeper into the complexities of character and politics in this violent episode of Rome's history. It can be frustrating to be faced with a text where the author does not simply say what he means. In that respect, reading Tacitus' work is like reading poetry, where meaning is often obscured, or where the words yield more than one meaning. But Tacitus' purpose is more serious than much poetry, for he aims to train his readers in the art of looking behind the official versions of public events, and discerning the private self-interest that often drives political actions. This is a skill that is as relevant today as it was in the first century AD.

Further reading

Ash, Rhiannon. 1999. *Ordering Anarchy: Armies and Leaders in Tacitus' Histories*, London: an accessible and comprehensive study, showing how Tacitus' characterization of Galba and Otho differs from Plutarch's and Suetonius' versions, and draws on broader literary themes.

Ash, Rhiannon. 2006. *Tacitus*, London: a short and excellent overview of Tacitus' political and literary career, and the influence of his works.

Ash, Rhiannon. 2009. 'Fission and Fusion: Shifting Roman Identities in the *Histories*' in A.J. Woodman, ed. 2009. *The Cambridge Companion to Tacitus*, Cambridge, 85–99.

Birley, Anthony. 2000. 'The Life and Death of Cornelius Tacitus', *Historia* 49: 230–247.

Damon, Cynthia. 2003. *Tacitus: Histories Book I*, Cambridge: a detailed and excellent commentary on the whole of Book I, with useful introductions.

Devillers, Olivier. 2012. 'The Concentration of Power and Writing History: Histories 1.1–49' in Victoria Pagán, ed. *A Companion to Tacitus*, Malden, MA, 162–186.

Haynes, Holly. 2003. *The History of Make-Believe: Tacitus on Imperial Rome*, Berkeley, CA: a challenging and dense analysis of *Histories* as a whole; the focus on Book I is mostly on Galba's speech to Piso.

Keitel, Elizabeth. 2006. '*Sententia* and Structure in Tacitus *Histories* 1.12–49', *Arethusa* 39: 219–244.

Levene, David S. 1999. 'Tacitus' *Histories* and the Theory of Deliberative Oratory' in Christina Shuttleworth Kraus, ed. *The Limits of Historiography: Genre and Narrative in Ancient Historical Texts*, Leiden, 197–216.

Morgan, M. Gwyn. 2006. *69. A.D.: The Year of Four Emperors*, Oxford: the best history of the civil war, which also provides a good model for how to use Tacitus as a historical source.

Pomeroy, Arthur. 2006. 'Theatricality in Tacitus's *Histories*', *Arethusa* 39: 171–191.

Sailor, Dylan. 2008. *Writing and Empire in Tacitus*, Cambridge: on Tacitus' works as a whole; the chapters on *Histories* focus mostly on the preface and Otho's speeches.

Syme, Ronald. 1958. *Tacitus*, 2 vols. Oxford: a comprehensive analysis of Tacitus' life and works, including detailed political analyses of the Julio-Claudian, Flavian, and early Antonine dynasties. The appendices include useful reviews of Tacitus' word-choice across the different works.

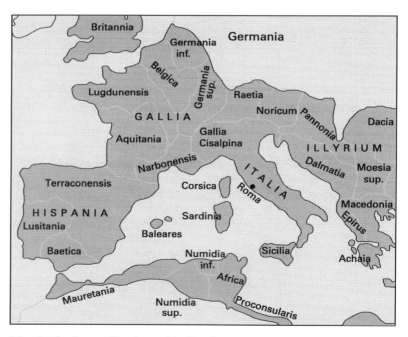

Map 1 The Roman Empire and its Provinces in AD 69

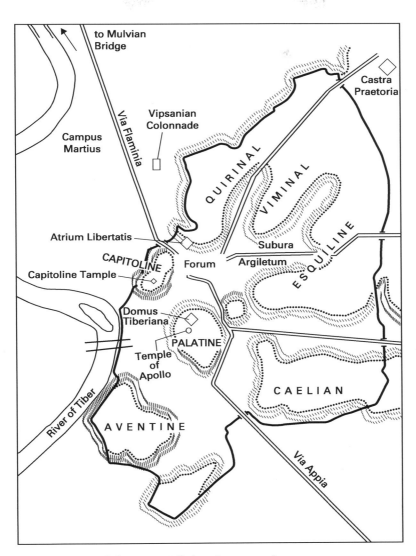

Map 2 Rome and the Seven Hills (1st Century AD)

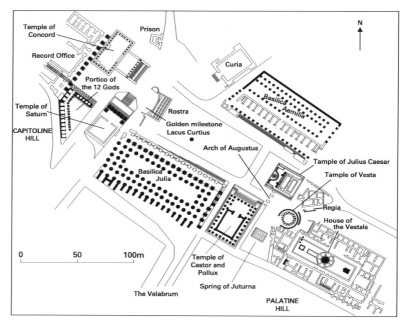

Map 3 The Roman Forum (1st Century AD)

Timeline

AD 54	Accession of Nero, the last Julio-Claudian emperor.
56 or 58	Birth of Tacitus.
58	Nero sends Otho to Lusitania, and begins an affair with Poppaea.
62	Nero exiles and kills his wife Octavia, and marries Poppaea.
65	Death of Poppaea.
	A conspiracy against Nero is uncovered, and many Roman senators, equestrians and soldiers are executed.
68	Revolt of Julius Vindex, governor of Gallia Lugdunensis. After Vindex's defeat, other rebellions arise, including that of Galba, governor of Spain.
	At Rome, the Praetorian Guard defects, and the senate declares Nero a public enemy. Nero takes his own life.
	Galba declared emperor by Senate.
	Death of Nymphidius Sabinus.
	Galba marches to Rome; massacre of marines at the Mulvian Bridge.
69	'The Year of Four Emperors'
January	Legions of the German provinces declare Vitellius emperor.
	At Rome, Otho wins the support of the Praetorian Guard; Galba is killed and Otho is ratified as emperor by the Senate.
March	Otho marches north to meet Vitellius' troops, where he is defeated and takes his own life. Vitellius is ratified as emperor by the senate.
June	Vitellius marches to Rome.
July	Vespasian is declared emperor by the legions in Egypt, Syria and Judaea.

August	Vespasian's generals gain support in Pannonia and march into northern Italy.
October	Vitellius' legions are defeated by Vespasian's generals.
December	As Vespasian's forces take control of Italy, Vitellius in Rome attempts to abdicate. Fighting reaches the city, and Vitellius' soldiers set fire to the Capitol. Vespasian's generals capture the city and Vitellius is executed.
70	Vespasian is ratified as emperor by the Senate.
	The Capitol is restored.
	Jerusalem is captured and its Temple destroyed.
76	Tacitus enters public life as a decemvir.
79	Death of Vespasian; accession of Titus.
	Eruption of Vesuvius at Pompeii.
81	Death of Titus; accession of Domitian.
82	Tacitus becomes quaestor.
88	Tacitus becomes praetor and member of a priestly college responsible for administering the secular games.
89–93	Tacitus serves abroad.
96	Domitian is assassinated by a small group of conspirators; Nerva is declared emperor by the senate.
97	Mutiny of the Praetorian Guard, demanding punishment of Domitian's assassins. Nerva announces the adoption of Trajan.
	Tacitus is consul in the last quarter of the year.
98	Death of Nerva; accession of Trajan.
	Tacitus publishes *Agricola* and *Germania*.
102 or 107	Likely publication date of *Dialogus de Oratoribus*.
109	Tacitus publishes *Historiae*.
112–113	Tacitus is governor of Asia.
117	Death of Trajan; accession of Hadrian.
After 117	Publication of *Annales*.
	Death of Tacitus.

Text

4.2 finis Neronis ut laetus primo gaudentium impetu fuerat, ita varios motus animorum non modo in urbe apud patres aut populum aut urbanum militem, sed omnes legiones ducesque conciverat, evulgato imperii arcano posse principem alibi quam Romae fieri. sed 3 patres laeti, usurpata statim libertate licentius ut erga principem novum et absentem; primores equitum proximi gaudio patrum; pars populi integra et magnis domibus adnexa, clientes libertique damnatorum et exulum in spem erecti: plebs sordida et circo ac theatris sueta, simul deterrimi servorum, aut qui adesis bonis per dedecus Neronis alebantur, maesti et rumorum avidi.

5. miles urbanus longo Caesarum sacramento imbutus et ad destituendum Neronem arte magis et impulsu quam suo ingenio traductus, postquam neque dari donativum sub nomine Galbae promissum neque magnis meritis ac praemiis eundem in pace quem in bello locum praeventamque gratiam intellegit apud principem a legionibus factum, pronus ad novas res scelere insuper Nymphidii Sabini praefecti imperium sibi molientis agitatur. et Nymphidius 2 quidem in ipso conatu oppressus, set quamvis capite defectionis ablato manebat plerisque militum conscientia, nec deerant sermones senium atque avaritiam Galbae increpantium. laudata olim et militari fama celebrata severitas eius angebat aspernantes veterem disciplinam atque ita quattuordecim annis a Nerone adsuefactos ut haud minus vitia principum amarent quam olim virtutes verebantur. accessit Galbae vox pro re publica honesta, ipsi anceps, legi a se militem, non emi; nec enim ad hanc formam cetera erant.

6. invalidum senem Titus Vinius et Cornelius Laco, alter deterrimus mortalium, alter ignavissimus, odio flagitiorum oneratum contemptu inertiae destruebant. tardum Galbae iter et cruentum, interfectis Cingonio Varrone consule designato et Petronio Turpiliano consulari: ille ut Nymphidii socius, hic ut dux Neronis, inauditi atque indefensi tamquam innocentes perierant. introitus in urbem trucidatis tot 2 milibus inermium militum infaustus omine atque ipsis etiam qui occiderant formidolosus. inducta legione Hispana, remanente ea quam e classe Nero conscripserat, plena urbs exercitu insolito; multi ad hoc numeri e Germania ac Britannia et Illyrico, quos idem Nero electos praemissosque ad claustra Caspiarum et bellum, quod in Albanos parabat, opprimendis Vindicis coeptis revocaverat: ingens novis rebus materia, ut non in unum aliquem prono favore ita audenti parata.

7.   forte congruerat ut Clodii Macri et Fontei Capitonis caedes nuntiarentur. Macrum in Africa haud dubie turbantem Trebonius Garutianus procurator iussu Galbae, Capitonem in Germania, cum similia coeptaret, Cornelius Aquinus et Fabius Valens legati legionum interfecerant antequam iuberentur. fuere qui crederent Capitonem ut 2 avaritia et libidine foedum ac maculosum ita cogitatione rerum novarum abstinuisse, sed a legatis bellum suadentibus, postquam impellere nequiverint, crimen ac dolum ultro compositum, et Galbam mobilitate ingenii, an ne altius scrutaretur, quoquo modo acta, quia mutari non poterant, comprobasse. ceterum utraque caedes sinistre accepta, et inviso semel principi seu bene seu male facta parem invidiam adferebant. venalia cuncta, praepotentes liberti, servorum 3 manus subitis avidae et tamquam apud senem festinantes, eademque novae aulae mala, aeque gravia, non aeque excusata. ipsa aetas Galbae inrisui ac fastidio erat adsuetis iuventae Neronis et imperatores forma ac decore corporis, ut est mos vulgi, comparantibus.

Chapters 8–11: Tacitus now considers the state of affairs outside Rome. Most worrying are the feelings among the German legions, who are described as anxious and angry. Tacitus also names the future emperors

Vitellius, who Galba has sent to command the disaffected troops in Lower Germany, and Vespasian, who is fighting a war against the Jews. He ends by darkly foreshadowing the death of Galba and the near destruction of the Roman state.

12. paucis post kalendas Ianuarias diebus Pompei Propinqui procuratoris e Belgica litterae adferuntur, superioris Germaniae legiones rupta sacramenti reverentia imperatorem alium flagitare et senatui ac populo Romano arbitrium eligendi permittere quo seditio mollius acciperetur. maturavit ea res consilium Galbae iam pridem de   2 adoptione secum et cum proximis agitantis. non sane crebrior tota civitate sermo per illos menses fuerat, primum licentia ac libidine talia loquendi, dein fessa iam aetate Galbae. paucis iudicium aut rei   3 publicae amor: multi stulta spe, prout quis amicus vel cliens, hunc vel illum ambitiosis rumoribus destinabant, etiam in Titi Vinii odium, qui in dies quanto potentior eodem actu invisior erat. quippe hiantes in magna fortuna amicorum cupiditates ipsa Galbae facilitas intendebat, cum apud infirmum et credulum minore metu et maiore praemio peccaretur.

13. potentia principatus divisa in Titum Vinium consulem Cornelium Laconem praetorii praefectum; nec minor gratia Icelo Galbae liberto, quem anulis donatum equestri nomine Marcianum vocitabant. hi discordes et rebus minoribus sibi quisque tendentes, circa consilium eligendi successoris in duas factiones scindebantur. Vinius pro M. Othone, Laco atque Icelus consensu non tam unum   2 aliquem fovebant quam alium. neque erat Galbae ignota Othonis ac Titi Vinii amicitia; et rumoribus nihil silentio transmittentium, quia Vinio vidua filia, caelebs Otho, gener ac socer destinabantur. credo et rei publicae curam subisse, frustra a Nerone translatae si apud Othonem relinqueretur. namque Otho pueritiam incuriose,   3 adulescentiam petulanter egerat, gratus Neroni aemulatione luxus. eoque Poppaeam Sabinam, principale scortum, ut apud conscium

AS

libidinum deposuerat, donec Octaviam uxorem amoliretur. mox suspectum in eadem Poppaea in provinciam Lusitaniam specie legationis seposuit. Otho comiter administrata provincia primus in 4 partes transgressus nec segnis et, donec bellum fuit, inter praesentes splendidissimus, spem adoptionis statim conceptam acrius in dies rapiebat, faventibus plerisque militum, prona in eum aula Neronis ut similem.

14. sed Galba post nuntios Germanicae seditionis, quamquam nihil adhuc de Vitellio certum, anxius quonam exercituum vis erumperet, ne urbano quidem militi confisus, quod remedium unicum rebatur, comitia imperii transigit; adhibitoque super Vinium ac Laconem Mario Celso consule designato ac Ducenio Gemino praefecto urbis, pauca praefatus de sua senectute, Pisonem Licinianum accersiri iubet, seu propria electione sive, ut quidam crediderunt, Lacone instante, cui apud Rubellium Plautum exercita cum Pisone amicitia; sed callide ut ignotum fovebat, et prospera de Pisone fama consilio eius fidem addiderat. Piso M. Crasso et Scribonia genitus, nobilis utrimque, vultu 2 habituque moris antiqui et aestimatione recta severus, deterius interpretantibus tristior habebatur: ea pars morum eius quo suspectior sollicitis adoptanti placebat.

Chapters 15–16: After taking Piso by the hand, Galba addresses him in direct speech. This marks the adoption of Piso, but Galba also justifies adoption as a mode of succession, praises Piso's qualities and advises him on how to govern. The very personal and private nature of the first speech in the Histories *is notably different from the grand, public set speeches that are common in historians of earlier periods.*

17. Pisonem ferunt statim intuentibus et mox coniectis in eum omnium oculis nullum turbati aut exultantis animi motum prodidisse. sermo erga patrem imperatoremque reverens, de se moderatus; nihil in vultu habituque mutatum, quasi imperare posset magis quam vellet. consultatum inde, pro rostris an in senatu an in castris adoptio 2 nuncuparetur. iri in castra placuit: honorificum id militibus fore, quorum favorem ut largitione et ambitu male adquiri, ita per bonas artes haud spernendum. circumsteterat interim Palatium publica expectatio, magni secreti impatiens; et male coercitam famam supprimentes augebant.

18. quartum idus Ianuarias, foedum imbribus diem, tonitrua et fulgura et caelestes minae ultra solitum turbaverunt. observatum id antiquitus comitiis dirimendis non terruit Galbam quo minus in castra pergeret, contemptorem talium ut fortuitorum; seu quae fato manent, quamvis significata, non vitantur. apud frequentem militum 2 contionem imperatoria brevitate adoptari a se Pisonem exemplo divi Augusti et more militari, quo vir virum legeret, pronuntiat. ac ne dissimulata seditio in maius crederetur, ultro adseverat quartam et duoetvicensimam legiones, paucis seditionis auctoribus, non ultra verba ac voces errasse et brevi in officio fore. nec ullum orationi aut lenocinium addit aut pretium. tribuni tamen centurionesque et 3 proximi militum grata auditu respondent: per ceteros maestitia ac silentium, tamquam usurpatam etiam in pace donativi necessitatem bello perdidissent. constat potuisse conciliari animos quantulacumque parci senis liberalitate: nocuit antiquus rigor et nimia severitas, cui iam pares non sumus.

19. inde apud senatum non comptior Galbae, non longior quam apud militem sermo: Pisonis comis oratio. et patrum favor aderat: multi voluntate, effusius qui noluerant, medii ac plurimi obvio obsequio, privatas spes agitantes sine publica cura. nec aliud sequenti quadriduo, quod medium inter adoptionem et caedem fuit, dictum a Pisone in publico factumve. crebrioribus in dies Germanicae 2 defectionis nuntiis et facili civitate ad accipienda credendaque omnia nova cum tristia sunt, censuerant patres mittendos ad Germanicum exercitum legatos. agitatum secreto num et Piso proficisceretur, maiore praetextu, illi auctoritatem senatus, hic dignationem Caesaris laturus. placebat et Laconem praetorii praefectum simul mitti: is consilio intercessit. legati quoque (nam senatus electionem Galbae permiserat) foeda inconstantia nominati, excusati, substituti, ambitu remanendi aut eundi, ut quemque metus vel spes impulerat.

20.   proxima pecuniae cura; et cuncta scrutantibus iustissimum visum est inde repeti ubi inopiae causa erat. bis et viciens miliens sestertium donationibus Nero effuderat: appellari singulos iussit, decima parte liberalitatis apud quemque eorum relicta. at illis vix decimae super portiones erant, isdem erga aliena sumptibus quibus sua prodegerant, cum rapacissimo cuique ac perditissimo non agri aut faenus sed sola instrumenta vitiorum manerent. exactioni triginta   2 equites Romani praepositi, novum officii genus et ambitu ac numero onerosum: ubique hasta et sector, et inquieta urbs actionibus. ac tamen grande gaudium quod tam pauperes forent quibus donasset Nero quam quibus abstulisset. exauctorati per eos dies tribuni, e   3 praetorio Antonius Taurus et Antonius Naso, ex urbanis cohortibus Aemilius Pacensis, e vigilibus Iulius Fronto. nec remedium in ceteros fuit, sed metus initium, tamquam per artem et formidine singuli pellerentur, omnibus suspectis.

21.   interea Othonem, cui compositis rebus nulla spes, omne in turbido consilium, multa simul extimulabant, luxuria etiam principi onerosa, inopia vix privato toleranda, in Galbam ira, in Pisonem invidia; fingebat et metum quo magis concupisceret: praegravem se Neroni fuisse, nec Lusitaniam rursus et alterius exilii honorem expectandum. suspectum semper invisumque dominantibus qui proximus destinaretur. nocuisse id sibi apud senem principem, magis nociturum apud iuvenem ingenio trucem et longo exilio efferatum: occidi Othonem posse. proinde agendum audendumque, dum Galbae   2 auctoritas fluxa, Pisonis nondum coaluisset. opportunos magnis conatibus transitus rerum, nec cunctatione opus, ubi perniciosior sit quies quam temeritas. mortem omnibus ex natura aequalem oblivione apud posteros vel gloria distingui; ac si nocentem innocentemque idem exitus maneat, acrioris viri esse merito perire.

22. non erat Othonis mollis et corpori similis animus. et intimi libertorum servorumque, corruptius quam in privata domo habiti, aulam Neronis et luxus, adulteria, matrimonia ceterasque regnorum libidines avido talium, si auderet, ut sua ostentantes, quiescenti ut aliena exprobrabant, urgentibus etiam mathematicis, dum novos motus et clarum Othoni annum observatione siderum adfirmant, genus hominum potentibus infidum, sperantibus fallax, quod in civitate nostra et vetabitur semper et retinebitur. multos secreta   2 Poppaeae mathematicos, pessimum principalis matrimonii instrumentum, habuerant: e quibus Ptolemaeus Othoni in Hispania comes, cum superfuturum eum Neroni promisisset, postquam ex eventu fides, coniectura iam et rumore senium Galbae et iuventam Othonis computantium persuaserat fore ut in imperium adscisceretur. sed Otho tamquam peritia et monitu fatorum praedicta accipiebat,   3 cupidine ingenii humani libentius obscura credendi. nec deerat Ptolemaeus, iam et sceleris instinctor, ad quod facillime ab eius modi voto transitur.

23. sed sceleris cogitatio incertum an repens: studia militum iam pridem spe successionis aut paratu facinoris adfectaverat, in itinere, in agmine, in stationibus vetustissimum quemque militum nomine vocans ac memoria Neroniani comitatus contubernales appellando; alios agnoscere, quosdam requirere et pecunia aut gratia iuvare, inserendo saepius querelas et ambiguos de Galba sermones quaeque alia turbamenta vulgi. labores itinerum, inopia commeatuum, duritia   2 imperii atrocius accipiebantur, cum Campaniae lacus et Achaiae urbes classibus adire soliti Pyrenaeum et Alpes et immensa viarum spatia aegre sub armis eniterentur.

AS

Chapters 24–25: Tacitus relates some instances of Otho's bribery of the praetorians. Otho then entrusts the plot to his freedman Onomastus, who uses two members of the guard to stir up the soldiers' anxieties.

26.   infecit ea tabes legionum quoque et auxiliorum motas iam mentes, postquam vulgatum erat labare Germanici exercitus fidem. adeoque parata apud malos seditio, etiam apud integros dissimulatio fuit, ut postero iduum die redeuntem a cena Othonem rapturi fuerint, ni incerta noctis et tota urbe sparsa militum castra nec facilem inter temulentos consensum timuissent, non rei publicae cura, quam foedare principis sui sanguine sobrii parabant, sed ne per tenebras, ut quisque Pannonici vel Germanici exercitus militibus oblatus esset, ignorantibus plerisque, pro Othone destinaretur. multa erumpentis   2 seditionis indicia per conscios oppressa: quaedam apud Galbae aures praefectus Laco elusit, ignarus militarium animorum consiliique quamvis egregii, quod non ipse adferret, inimicus et adversus peritos pervicax.

27. octavo decimo kalendas Februarias sacrificanti pro aede Apollinis Galbae haruspex Umbricius tristia exta et instantes insidias ac domesticum hostem praedicit, audiente Othone (nam proximus adstiterat) idque ut laetum e contrario et suis cogitationibus prosperum interpretante. nec multo post libertus Onomastus nuntiat expectari eum ab architecto et redemptoribus, quae significatio coeuntium iam militum et paratae coniurationis convenerat. Otho, causam digressus requirentibus, cum emi sibi praedia vetustate suspecta eoque prius exploranda finxisset, innixus liberto per Tiberianam domum in Velabrum, inde ad miliarium aureum sub aedem Saturni pergit. ibi tres et viginti speculatores consalutatum imperatorem ac paucitate salutantium trepidum et sellae festinanter impositum strictis mucronibus rapiunt; totidem ferme milites in itinere adgregantur, alii conscientia, plerique miraculo, pars clamore et gladiis, pars silentio, animum ex eventu sumpturi.

28. stationem in castris agebat Iulius Martialis tribunus. is magnitudine subiti sceleris, an corrupta latius castra et, si contra tenderet, exitium metuens, praebuit plerisque suspicionem conscientiae; anteposuere ceteri quoque tribuni centurionesque praesentia dubiis et honestis, isque habitus animorum fuit ut pessimum facinus auderent pauci, plures vellent, omnes paterentur.

29. ignarus interim Galba et sacris intentus fatigabat alieni iam imperii deos, cum adfertur rumor rapi in castra incertum quem senatorem, mox Othonem esse qui raperetur, simul ex tota urbe, ut quisque obvius fuerat, alii formidine augentes, quidam minora vero, ne tum quidem obliti adulationis. igitur consultantibus placuit pertemptari animum cohortis, quae in Palatio stationem agebat, nec per ipsum Galbam, cuius integra auctoritas maioribus remediis servabatur. Piso pro gradibus domus vocatos in hunc modum adlocutus est: 'sextus dies agitur, commilitones, ex quo ignarus futuri, et sive optandum hoc nomen sive timendum erat, Caesar adscitus

A Level

sum. quo domus nostrae aut rei publicae fato in vestra manu positum est, non quia meo nomine tristiorem casum paveam, ut qui adversas res expertus cum maxime discam ne secundas quidem minus discriminis habere: patris et senatus et ipsius imperii vicem doleo, si nobis aut perire hodie necesse est aut, quod aeque apud bonos miserum est, occidere. solacium proximi motus habebamus incruentam urbem et res sine discordia translatas: provisum adoptione videbatur ut ne post Galbam quidem bello locus esset.'

30. 'nihil adrogabo mihi nobilitatis aut modestiae; neque enim relatu virtutum in comparatione Othonis opus est. vitia, quibus solis gloriatur, evertere imperium, etiam cum amicum imperatoris ageret. habitune et incessu an illo muliebri ornatu mereretur imperium? falluntur quibus luxuria specie liberalitatis imponit: perdere iste sciet, donare nesciet. stupra nunc et comissationes et feminarum coetus volvit animo: haec principatus praemia putat, quorum libido ac voluptas penes ipsum sit, rubor ac dedecus penes omnes; nemo enim umquam imperium flagitio quaesitum bonis artibus exercuit. Galbam consensus generis humani,   2 me Galba consentientibus vobis Caesarem dixit. si res publica et senatus et populus vacua nomina sunt, vestra, commilitones, interest ne imperatorem pessimi faciant. legionum seditio adversus duces suos audita est aliquando: vestra fides famaque inlaesa ad hunc diem mansit. et Nero quoque vos destituit, non vos Neronem. minus triginta   3 transfugae et desertores, quos centurionem aut tribunum sibi eligentes nemo ferret, imperium adsignabunt? admittitis exemplum et quiescendo commune crimen facitis? transcendet haec licentia in provincias, et ad nos scelerum exitus, bellorum ad vos pertinebunt. nec est plus quod pro caede principis quam quod innocentibus datur, sed proinde a nobis donativum ob fidem quam ab aliis pro facinore accipietis.'

31. dilapsis speculatoribus cetera cohors non aspernata contionantem, ut turbidis rebus evenit, forte magis et nullo adhuc consilio rapit signa quam, quod postea creditum est, insidiis et

**A
Level**

simulatione. missus et Celsus Marius ad electos Illyrici exercitus, 2
Vipsania in porticu tendentes; praeceptum Amullio Sereno et Domitio
Sabino primipilaribus, ut Germanicos milites e Libertatis atrio
accerserent. legioni classicae diffidebatur, infestae ob caedem
commilitonum, quos primo statim introitu trucidaverat Galba. pergunt
etiam in castra praetorianorum tribuni Cetrius Severus, Subrius
Dexter, Pompeius Longinus, si incipiens adhuc et necdum adulta
seditio melioribus consiliis flecteretur. tribunorum Subrium et Cetrium 3
adorti milites minis, Longinum manibus coercent exarmantque, quia
non ordine militiae, sed e Galbae amicis, fidus principi suo et
desciscentibus suspectior erat. legio classica nihil cunctata praetorianis
adiungitur; Illyrici exercitus electi Celsum infestis pilis proturbant.
Germanica vexilla diu nutavere, invalidis adhuc corporibus et placatis
animis, quod eos a Nerone Alexandriam praemissos atque inde rursus
longa navigatione aegros impensiore cura Galba refovebat.

32. universa iam plebs Palatium implebat, mixtis servitiis et dissono
clamore caedem Othonis et coniuratorum exitium poscentium
ut si in circo aut theatro ludicrum aliquod postularent: neque illis
iudicium aut veritas, quippe eodem die diversa pari certamine
postulaturis, sed tradito more quemcumque principem adulandi
licentia adclamationum et studiis inanibus.

interim Galbam duae sententiae distinebant: Titus Vinius manendum 2
intra domum, opponenda servitia, firmandos aditus, non eundum ad
iratos censebat: daret malorum paenitentiae, daret bonorum consensui
spatium: scelera impetu, bona consilia mora valescere, denique eundi
ultro, si ratio sit, eandem mox facultatem, regressum, si paeniteat, in
aliena potestate.

33. festinandum ceteris videbatur antequam cresceret invalida
adhuc coniuratio paucorum: trepidaturum etiam Othonem, qui
furtim digressus, ad ignaros inlatus, cunctatione nunc et segnitia
terentium tempus imitari principem discat. non expectandum ut

**A
Level**

compositis castris forum invadat et prospectante Galba Capitolium adeat, dum egregius imperator cum fortibus amicis ianua ac limine tenus domum cludit, obsidionem nimirum toleraturus. et praeclarum 2 in servis auxilium si consensus tantae multitudinis et, quae plurimum valet, prima indignatio elanguescat. proinde intuta quae indecora; vel si cadere necesse sit, occurrendum discrimini: id Othoni invidiosius et ipsis honestum. repugnantem huic sententiae Vinium Laco minaciter invasit, stimulante Icelo privati odii pertinacia in publicum exitium.

34.   nec diutius Galba cunctatus speciosiora suadentibus accessit. praemissus tamen in castra Piso, ut iuvenis magno nomine, recenti favore et infensus Tito Vinio, seu quia erat seu quia irati ita volebant; et facilius de odio creditur. vixdum egresso Pisone occisum in castris 2 Othonem vagus primum et incertus rumor: mox, ut in magnis mendaciis, interfuisse se quidam et vidisse adfirmabant, credula fama inter gaudentes et incuriosos. multi arbitrabantur compositum auctumque rumorem mixtis iam Othonianis, qui ad evocandum Galbam laeta falso vulgaverint.

35.   tum vero non populus tantum et imperita plebs in plausus et immodica studia sed equitum plerique ac senatorum, posito metu incauti, refractis Palatii foribus ruere intus ac se Galbae ostentare, praereptam sibi ultionem querentes, ignavissimus quisque et, ut res docuit, in periculo non ausurus, nimii verbis, linguae feroces; nemo scire et omnes adfirmare, donec inopia veri et consensu errantium victus sumpto thorace Galba inruenti turbae neque aetate neque corpore resistens sella levaretur. obvius in Palatio Iulius Atticus 2 speculator, cruentum gladium ostentans, occisum a se Othonem exclamavit; et Galba 'commilito', inquit, 'quis iussit?' insigni animo ad coercendam militarem licentiam, minantibus intrepidus, adversus blandientes incorruptus.

36.   haud dubiae iam in castris omnium mentes tantusque ardor ut non contenti agmine et corporibus in suggestu, in quo paulo ante

A
Level

aurea Galbae statua fuerat, medium inter signa Othonem vexillis circumdarent. nec tribunis aut centurionibus adeundi locus: gregarius miles caveri insuper praepositos iubebat. strepere cuncta clamoribus 2 et tumultu et exhortatione mutua, non tamquam in populo ac plebe, variis segni adulatione vocibus, sed ut quemque adfluentium militum aspexerant, prensare manibus, complecti armis, conlocare iuxta, praeire sacramentum, modo imperatorem militibus, modo milites imperatori commendare. nec deerat Otho protendens manus adorare 3 vulgum, iacere oscula et omnia serviliter pro dominatione. postquam universa classicorum legio sacramentum eius accepit, fidens viribus, et quos adhuc singulos extimulaverat, accendendos in commune ratus pro vallo castrorum ita coepit.

Chapters 37–38: Otho's speech to the soldiers begins by stressing how their fates are now tied. He recalls Galba's slaughter of the marines and the unpaid donative, criticizes Vinius and Piso, and claims that the senate and the Roman people are depending on them. The speech also describes how Galba has subverted language, calling his punishments 'discipline', his cruelty 'strictness', and his greed 'frugality'. Here Tacitus shows a keen understanding of the importance of language as an instrument of political control, and of the way in which it is contested by people with different claims to power.

At the end of chapter 38 Otho orders the armoury to be opened. Tacitus provides a fabulous description of the soldiers wildly rushing to arms that captures perfectly the disintegration of military order.

39.   iam exterritus Piso fremitu crebrescentis seditionis et vocibus in urbem usque resonantibus, egressum interim Galbam et foro adpropinquantem adsecutus erat; iam Marius Celsus haud laeta rettulerat, cum alii in Palatium redire, alii Capitolium petere, plerique rostra occupanda censerent, plures tantum sententiis aliorum contra dicerent, utque evenit in consiliis infelicibus, optima viderentur quorum tempus effugerat. agitasse Laco ignaro Galba de occidendo Tito Vinio 2

**A
Level**

dicitur, sive ut poena eius animos militum mulceret, seu conscium Othonis credebat, ad postremum vel odio. haesitationem attulit tempus ac locus, quia initio caedis orto difficilis modus; et turbavere consilium trepidi nuntii ac proximorum diffugia, languentibus omnium studiis qui primo alacres fidem atque animum ostentaverant.

40. agebatur huc illuc Galba vario turbae fluctuantis impulsu, completis undique basilicis ac templis, lugubri prospectu. neque populi aut plebis ulla vox, sed attoniti vultus et conversae ad omnia aures; non tumultus, non quies, quale magni metus et magnae irae silentium est. Othoni tamen armari plebem nuntiabatur; ire praecipites et occupare pericula iubet. igitur milites Romani, quasi Vologaesum aut Pacorum   2 avito Arsacidarum solio depulsuri ac non imperatorem suum inermem et senem trucidare pergerent, disiecta plebe, proculcato senatu, truces armis, rapidi equis forum inrumpunt. nec illos Capitolii aspectus et imminentium templorum religio et priores et futuri principes terruere quo minus facerent scelus cuius ultor est quisquis successit.

41. viso comminus armatorum agmine vexillarius comitatae Galbam cohortis (Atilium Vergilionem fuisse tradunt) dereptam Galbae imaginem solo adflixit: eo signo manifesta in Othonem omnium militum studia, desertum fuga populi forum, destricta adversus dubitantes tela. iuxta Curtii lacum trepidatione ferentium   2 Galba proiectus e sella ac provolutus est. extremam eius vocem, ut cuique odium aut admiratio fuit, varie prodidere. alii suppliciter interrogasse quid mali meruisset, paucos dies exolvendo donativo deprecatum: plures obtulisse ultro percussoribus iugulum: agerent ac ferirent, si ita e re publica videretur. non interfuit occidentium quid diceret. de percussore non satis constat: quidam Terentium evocatum,   3 alii Laecanium; crebrior fama tradidit Camurium quintae decimae legionis militem impresso gladio iugulum eius hausisse. ceteri crura brachiaque (nam pectus tegebatur) foede laniavere; pleraque vulnera feritate et saevitia trunco iam corpori adiecta.

A
Level

42. Titum inde Vinium invasere, de quo et ipso ambigitur consumpseritne vocem eius instans metus, an proclamaverit non esse ab Othone mandatum ut occideretur. quod seu finxit formidine seu conscientiam coniurationis confessus est, huc potius eius vita famaque inclinat, ut conscius sceleris fuerit cuius causa erat. ante aedem divi Iulii iacuit primo ictu in poplitem, mox ab Iulio Caro legionario milite in utrumque latus transverberatus.

43. insignem illa die virum Sempronium Densum aetas nostra vidit. centurio is praetoriae cohortis, a Galba custodiae Pisonis additus, stricto pugione occurrens armatis et scelus exprobrans ac modo manu modo voce vertendo in se percussores quamquam vulnerato Pisoni effugium dedit. Piso in aedem Vestae pervasit,   2 exceptusque misericordia publici servi et contubernio eius abditus non religione nec caerimoniis sed latebra inminens exitium differebat, cum advenere missu Othonis nominatim in caedem eius ardentis Sulpicius Florus e Britannicis cohortibus, nuper a Galba civitate donatus, et Statius Murcus speculator, a quibus protractus Piso in foribus templi trucidatur.

44. nullam caedem Otho maiore laetitia excepisse, nullum caput tam insatiabilibus oculis perlustrasse dicitur, seu tum primum levata omni sollicitudine mens vacare gaudio coeperat, seu recordatio maiestatis in Galba, amicitiae in Tito Vinio quamvis immitem animum imagine tristi confuderat, Pisonis ut inimici et aemuli caede laetari ius fasque credebat. praefixa contis capita gestabantur inter signa   2 cohortium iuxta aquilam legionis, certatim ostentantibus cruentas manus qui occiderant, qui interfuerant, qui vere qui falso ut pulchrum et memorabile facinus iactabant. plures quam centum viginti libellos praemium exposcentium ob aliquam notabilem illa die operam Vitellius postea invenit, omnesque conquiri et interfici iussit, non honori Galbae, sed tradito principibus more munimentum ad praesens, in posterum ultionem.

A Level

Chapters 45–48: Tacitus describes the immediate aftermath of the rebellion. There are numerous displays of flattery from the senate and the people, and the will of the soldiers reigns supreme. Laco is exiled then assassinated, and Icelus is publicly executed. Piso and Titus Vinius are both buried by their families, and Tacitus gives both an obituary in chapter 48.

49. Galbae corpus diu neglectum et licentia tenebrarum plurimis ludibriis vexatum dispensator Argius e prioribus servis humili sepultura in privatis eius hortis contexit. caput per lixas calonesque suffixum laceratumque ante Patrobii tumulum (libertus is Neronis punitus a Galba fuerat) postera demum die repertum et cremato iam corpori admixtum est. hunc exitum habuit Servius Galba, tribus et   2
septuaginta annis quinque principes prospera fortuna emensus et alieno imperio felicior quam suo. vetus in familia nobilitas, magnae opes: ipsi medium ingenium, magis extra vitia quam cum virtutibus. famae nec incuriosus nec venditator; pecuniae alienae non adpetens,   3
suae parcus, publicae avarus; amicorum libertorumque, ubi in bonos incidisset, sine reprehensione patiens, si mali forent, usque ad culpam ignarus. sed claritas natalium et metus temporum obtentui, ut, quod segnitia erat, sapientia vocaretur. dum vigebat aetas militari laude   4
apud Germanias floruit. pro consule Africam moderate, iam senior citeriorem Hispaniam pari iustitia continuit, maior privato visus dum privatus fuit, et omnium consensu capax imperii nisi imperasset.

**A
Level**

Commentary Notes

Preface: Tacitus begins the Histories *with a short preface (Chapters 1–3) that outlines the themes and scope of his work. In Chapter 1 he assesses the condition of historical writing and its reception in the Principate (the period when the emperors ruled Rome), and expresses his own ambitions as a historian. Chapters 2–3 act as a dark table of contents, foreshadowing the deaths, wars, natural disasters, impiety and corruption that lie ahead for the reader, as well as mentioning a few virtuous acts for good measure.*

It is important to read these chapters carefully in English to get a good sense of Tacitus' aims and the flavour of the work to come. Such programmatic openings are an important feature of ancient historical writing, so in order to be best understood it should be read in conjunction with the beginnings of Tacitus' other historical works (Agricola, Annals) as well as those of other authors (Livy, Sallust, Herodotus, Thucydides).

Chapters 4–11 give an outline of the state of the empire as Galba comes to power, starting with the unstable conditions in Rome (4–7) and concluding with the provinces (8–11).

Chapter 4

4.2

ut ... ita ... – 'although ... nevertheless ...'. The subject of both clauses is *finis* ('the death').

laetus – not a 'happy' death but one that is 'welcome' or 'pleasing'.

primo gaudentium impetu – 'in the initial burst of people rejoicing'. The genitive present participle *gaudentium* focuses us on the people feeling the emotion (rather than just 'burst of joy') and the lack of noun in agreement gives a good example of the economy of style, or *brevitas*, that characterizes Tacitus' writing and gives such pace and excitement to the events. The word *impetus* (often elsewhere translated as 'attack') is also typical of Tacitus' selective use of vocabulary, conveying the intensity and speed of the people's reaction.

motus – accusative plural (fourth declension).

apud – a common preposition in Tacitus. Its basic meaning is that of proximity or presence, but this extends from physical presence to the presence in the mind of emotions or dispositions. A few examples from this selection should illustrate its wide range of reference: under (a leader) (7.3); into the keeping of (13.3); at the house of (14.1); in the presence of (18.2); to (19.1); with (20.1); among (26.1); in the eyes of (29.2); in (49.4).

patres – 'senators'. This title was thought to have derived from Romulus' legendary foundation of the senate from the heads of a hundred of Rome's leading families.

urbanum militem – *miles* is used in the singular here as a collective noun: 'the urban soldiery'. This refers primarily to the Praetorian Guard, the only troops stationed permanently in Rome. They were an elite group whose main role was to protect the emperor, as well as suppress riots and plots. They were also of great political importance in the Principate, involved, for example, in the assassination of Caligula and the declaration of Claudius as emperor (AD 41). The reference here may also include the urban cohorts that acted as Rome's police force from the time of Augustus, and were stationed in the *castra praetoria* along with the Praetorian Guard.

sed – 'but also'. The following accusatives are still governed by *apud*.

evulgato imperii arcano – in Classical Latin (Cicero and Caesar, for example) sentences are usually constructed as 'periods', beginning with a subject and ending with the main verb, with subordinate

AS

clauses placed in between. Tacitus, however, often adds unexpected details by placing subordinate constructions after the main verb (the 'appendix' sentence) as here with the addition of the ablative absolute and its dependent accusative and infinitive (*posse principem . . . fieri*). This gives it an arresting position, strengthening the notion that the secret is out and that the game has changed.

alibi quam Romae – the implication is 'by the legions'. Galba had been proclaimed emperor by his troops in Spain in AD 68, but previously the Praetorian Guard in Rome had been the only troops to declare an emperor (see above). *Romae* is locative.

4.3

patres laeti – supply *erant*. Tacitus misses out parts of *sum* more often than other authors. This increases the pace, and also throws more emphasis onto the word from which it is missing (here the adjective *laeti*).

usurpata statim libertate licentius – 'immediately enjoying their freedom with less restraint'. With the *princeps* absent the senators are able to exercise more independence in expressing their opinions and making decisions.

ut erga – 'as (was natural) towards'.

primores equitum – 'the foremost members of the equestrian class'. The *equites* were the lower of the two aristocratic classes (after the *senatores*) so named as they had made up the cavalry of early Rome.

proximi gaudio patrum – 'were nearly as joyful as the senators'. Literally 'closest to the joy of the senators'. *erant* should be supplied.

clientes – a 'client' was a free man who gave his loyalty and service to a patron (*patronus*) in return for benefits such as money, food or legal assistance.

AS

damnatorum et exulum – Galba presented himself as the saviour of the many condemned or exiled by Nero on charges of treason. They were pardoned and recalled, but on their return conflicts often arose with those who had profited from their absence.

erecti – supply *sunt*.

circo ac theatris sueta – chariot racing and drama were often financed by emperors, but Nero in particular had devoted great public expense to entertainment.

qui ... alebantur – supply *ei* as the antecedent of *qui* ('those who ...'). The words *alebantur* and *adesis* (*ad-edo* literally 'eat up') cast these men as parasites.

bonis – 'property' (cf. English 'goods').

maesti et rumorum avidi – supply *erant*.

Chapter 5

5.1

miles ... agitatur – a long periodic sentence (see n. 4.2 *evulgato*) starting with its subject and ending with the main verb. Between these two elements are two participle phrases (*imbutus ... traductus*), a temporal clause (*postquam ... factum*) containing three indirect statements dependent on *intellegit*, and an adjectival phrase (*pronus ... res*). This piling up of subordinate constructions before the main verb serves to give full explanation to the agitation of the praetorians.

miles urbanus – see n. 4.2 *urbanum*.

longo Caesarum sacramento imbutus – 'steeped in their long-standing oath to the Caesars'. A good example of Tacitus' use of metaphor: *imbuo* literally means 'drench', or 'wet', so its use suggests the depth of the soldiers' loyalty. The word *sacramentum* refers to the military oath of allegiance that makes the loyalty more tangible than if an abstract noun had been used (e.g. 'loyalty' or 'allegiance'), while *Caesar* is a common title for emperors, first used by Augustus in honour of Julius Caesar. Tacitus employs it here to remind us that Galba was the first emperor to be unrelated to Julius Caesar, and that as a result praetorian loyalty was not so guaranteed.

Caesarum – an 'objective genitive', as the Caesars are the object of the verbal idea contained in *sacramentum*, best rendered here as 'to'. The primary function of the genitive is to denote a relationship between nouns, which is often that of possession ('of'), but translations such as 'to', 'for' or 'with' are often more appropriate.

arte . . . et impulsu – 'by the artifice and instigation (of others)'.

donativum sub nomine Galbae promissum – a 'donative' was a gift of money given by an emperor to each soldier upon his accession or at other special occasions. The previous leader of the Praetorian Guard (the praetorian prefect), named Nymphidius Sabinus, had embraced Galba's cause for his own ends and offered this money on behalf of Galba. Plutarch (*Galba* 2) records the sum offered by Nymphidius as 7,500 drachmas (30,000 sesterces) for praetorians, and 1,250 drachmas (5,000 sesterces) for legionaries. These were vast sums of money: praetorians earned only 3,000 sesterces a year, and legionaries 900; it was double anything ever paid before; and, according to Plutarch, more than could be afforded. Galba, despite his wealth, refused even to pay them any money at all (see Chapter 18).

neque . . . eundem in pace quem in bello locum – 'nor was there the same room in peace as in war'. *esse* should be supplied. The relative pronoun *qui, quae, quod* may be used with *idem* to mean 'the same . . .

AS

as', and here it has been attracted into the same case as *locum* where one would expect the nominative *qui* – 'which (there is) in war'.

praeventam ... gratiam – 'the (chance of) favour was forestalled'. Supply *esse*.

apud principem a legionibus factum – again referring to the fact that Galba had been proclaimed emperor by his troops in Spain, and was therefore likely to favour them rather than the praetorians.

novas res – *res novae* ('new things') is a common term for 'revolution'.

Nymphidii Sabini praefecti imperium sibi molientis – when Nymphidius (see above) learnt that Galba had shown more favour to others (e.g. those catalogued in Chapter 6), he urged the praetorians to declare him emperor. They refused, and killed him before Galba arrived in Rome. Note the ironic juxtaposition of *praefecti imperium*.

5.2

oppressus – supply *est*.

set – alternative form of *sed*.

quamvis – 'although'. This qualifies the following ablative absolute, a usage rarely found in Classical Latin.

capite defectionis ablato – characteristically black Tacitean humour.

conscientia – 'guilty conscience'. Another feature of Tacitus' style is the propensity to use nouns where earlier authors prefer verbs. The employment of abstract nouns in particular, often as the subject of verbs, serves to expand the scope and frame of reference from the particular to the general. See also *severitas* in the next sentence.

senium – 'old age' (while *senum* is genitive plural of *senex* – 'old man').

increpantium – see n. 4.2 *primo*.

AS

militari fama celebrata – 'celebrated in the talk of the soldiers'.

aspernantes – supply *eos*.

ita quattuordecim annis a Nerone adsuefactos ut . . . – 'conditioned by Nero over fourteen years such that . . .', introducing a result clause.

verebantur – 'they respected'.

accessit Galbae vox – 'Added to this was the saying of Galba . . .'.

pro re publica honesta, ipsi anceps – notice the purposeful avoidance of balance in this contrast, where the first adjective is paired with a prepositional phrase and the second with a dative. This variation of expression is a stylistic feature known as *variatio*. The reader is forced to pay attention because Tacitus veers away from what one might expect. *re publica* here is not 'the Republic', but 'the state'.

legi a se militem, non emi – accusative and infinitive to report Galba's words. This saying is also related by Plutarch (*Galba* 18) and Suetonius (*Galba* 16).

nec enim ad hanc formam cetera erant – 'for everything else was not up to this standard'. *cetera* is somewhat vague and should be kept so in English. It may refer to Galba's own actions, which failed to live up to the standard he had set, but could also denote the general circumstances of the times, in which honourable intentions such as this were naive and ill-judged.

Chapter 6

6.1

invalidum senem – referring, as *oneratum* below, to Galba. Note the placement, which emphasizes Galba's vulnerability. Tacitus has a penchant for words with the negative suffix *in-*, suggesting a departure

AS

from an accepted standard. Chapter 6, for example, also contains *ignavissimus, inauditus, indefensus, innocens, inermis, infaustus* and *inertia*.

Titus Vinius – Galba's co-consul in AD 69. For a short biography see Chapter 48.

Cornelius Laco – appointed praetorian prefect by Galba after Nymphidius' execution.

odio flagitiorum oneratum contemptu inertiae – 'weighed down by (people's) hatred for the crimes (of the former and) by their scorn for the inactivity (of the latter)'. The parallel phrases *odio flagitiorum* and *contemptu inertiae* refer to Vinius and Laco respectively, repeating the antithesis expressed earlier by the superlatives. A few words need to be inserted in English, and the *brevitas* is heightened by *asyndeton*. *flagitiorum* and *inertiae* are both objective genitives (see n. 5.1 *Caesarum*).

tardum Galbae iter – supply *erat*. Galba had set out from Spain in July AD 68, and probably arrived in Rome in October.

Cingonio Varrone – consul-elect (*consule designato*) for AD 69, Cingonius Varro had composed the speech that Nymphidius had given to the praetorians to declare himself emperor.

Petronio Turpiliano – Petronius Turpilianus had been consul in AD 61. He was chosen by Nero as the general of the majority of the forces sent to crush Vindex and Galba, but his troops sided with Galba.

ille . . . hic . . . – 'the former . . . the latter'.

tamquam innocentes – 'as if they were innocent'. The point is not that they were actually innocent, but that they appeared innocent as a result of Galba's hastily misjudged actions. To put innocent people on trial draws attention to the lack of evidence against them, while guilty people may be tried openly and punished with legitimacy.

AS

6.2

introitus … infaustus omine – supply *erat* and translate as 'his entrance was ill-omened'. *omine* is an ablative of respect, modifying *infaustus* (literally 'inauspicious with respect to the omen').

trucidatis tot milibus inermium militum – on his return to Rome Galba was met at the Milvian Bridge by a large number of marines, who had been arranged into a legion by Nero, and were demanding that their status be upheld. Violence ensued and many were killed. Tacitus puts emphasis on the severity of Galba's action through the strong word *trucido* ('slaughter', 'massacre'), by exaggerating numbers, and with the detail *inermium*. Details, however, are hazy: Plutarch (*Galba* 15), for example, says that they were armed with swords and even that they were not marines, but praetorians.

inducta legione Hispana – the legion that Galba had formed in Spain to march on Rome (the *legio VII Gemina*, also known as the *VII Galbiana*).

plena urbs – supply *erat*. *plenus* here takes the ablative, but may also be followed by a genitive.

numeri – 'detachments' from the legions.

Illyrico – *Illyricum* (itself a province until AD 10) refers to the provinces of *Dalmatia* and *Pannonia*, an area that stretched from Croatia to Albania. For this and other places mentioned in the text, refer to the maps that are included after the Introduction.

idem – 'likewise'.

claustra Caspiarum – 'the Caspian Gates'. This is now known as the Darial Pass, and connects Georgia to Russia over the Caucusus mountains.

in Albanos – 'against the Albani', a tribe that lived on the west coast of the Caspian Sea. There is a possibility that Tacitus has confused this with the Alani, a nomadic tribe that lived north of the Caucusus Mountains.

opprimendis Vindicis coeptis – 'to crush Vindex's undertakings'. The dative gerundive is often used by Tacitus to express purpose, but rarely found in Classical Latin. Vindex, the governor of Gallia Lugdunensis, had revolted against Nero in AD 68, and had encouraged Galba to declare himself emperor. After his army was defeated by forces led by Verginius Rufus, he committed suicide.

ingens...parata – '(all these soldiers were) plentiful fuel for revolution, and although support did not yet incline to any individual, it was nevertheless available for someone daring'. The verb 'to be' should be supplied and *ut... ita* ('although...nevertheless') is used concessively (see n. 4.2 *ut*). The unbalanced pairing of the ablative phrase *prono favore* with the adjective *parata*, agreeing with *materia*, is an example of *variatio*.

Chapter 7

7.1

congruerat – used impersonally with the *ut* clause: 'at the same time it had happened that ...'.

Clodii Macri – Clodius Macer was the legionary commander in the rich province of Africa, which stretched along the North African coast from Algeria to Libya. He had revolted from Nero in AD 68 and cut off the corn supply from Rome. He then refused to recognize Galba, and showed ambitions for power by minting his own coins and raising a new legion.

Fontei Capitonis – Capito was consul in AD 67 and governor of Lower Germany.

Trebonius Garutianus procurator – *procuratores* were officials employed by emperors for a range of tasks such as provincial administration, tax collection and management of imperial estates. Trebonius' name survives only for his role in Macer's death (see also Plutarch *Galba* 15).

Cornelius Aquinus et Fabius Valens legati legionum – a *legatus legionis* was the senior commander of a legion, usually subordinate to the governor of the province if multiple legions were stationed there (in one-legion provinces the governor usually also commanded the legion). Aquinus is only cited here, while Fabius Valens is an important figure in *Histories* I–III. In AD 68 he was a legionary commander in Lower Germany and supported Galba initially. However, when the troops refused to back Galba, he encouraged them to proclaim Vitellius as emperor in early January AD 69, and he was instrumental in the defeat of Otho at the first Battle of Bedriacum. When Vespasian had marched on Rome, he tried to flee but was captured and executed before the end of the year.

Macrum ... antequam iuberentur – the main verb *interfecerant* should be taken with both subjects. Note also the parallel structure: each half of the sentence begins with the name of the executed, followed by the location and their actions, before giving the names of the executioners and their positions, and then finally addressing whether it had been sanctioned by Galba. There is also *variatio*: the participle *turbantem* matches the temporal clause *cum ... coeptaret*; and the ablative phrase *iussu Galbae* corresponds with the temporal clause *antequam iuberentur*. The syntax draws attention to certain similarities but also highlights the differences between the clear cut nature of Macer's case, and the imprecise details surrounding Capito.

antequam iuberentur – in Classical Latin the subjunctive is only used in temporal clauses when there is an added idea of purpose

AS

(*Oxford Latin Grammar*, pp. 118–119) but this ceases to be true in Silver Latin.

7.2

fuere ... comprobasse – a particularly long and complex sentence. Break it down by observing that *crederent* governs three accusative and infinitive constructions: *Capitonem ... abstinuisse, crimen ... compositum* (supply *esse*) and *Galbam ... comprobasse*. As often, the convoluted syntax reflects the meaning, highlighting the confusion and uncertainty around Capito's execution.

fuere qui crederent – 'there were some who believed ...'. *fuere* is an archaic form of *fuerunt*, and there is an implied *ei* ('those', 'some'), the natural correlative of *qui*. The subjunctive *crederent* is used because the relative clause is generic, and does not refer to specific individuals. This stands in contrast to the *haud dubie* used of Macer earlier.

ut ... ita – concessive (see n. 4.2 *ut*).

avaritia et libidine foedum ac maculosum – 'disgraceful and stained with greed and lust'.

postquam ... nequiverint – the subjunctive is used in subordinate clauses within indirect speech (suboblique clauses). However, note that the subjunctive is perfect, rather than following the strict rules of sequence which would require a pluperfect (*Oxford Latin Grammar*, pp. 86–87). This is a figure of speech known as *repraesentatio* which is more vivid as it presents events from the perspective of those there at the time.

a legatis ... crimen ac dolum ultro compositum – make active to aid translation: 'that the commanders ... had fabricated a charge and even organized a plot'. Tacitean economy of expression is seen in the use of *compositum* with each noun in different senses. Some translators take *crimen ac dolum* as *hendiadys* ('treacherous charge'), but the context shows that they refer to two separate actions: the *crimen* denotes the false accusation that Capito was stirring up revolution, and the *dolum* their plot to murder him (*Galbam ... comprobasse*).

ultro – may be used to denote an action which goes beyond what is expected and is best taken here as 'furthermore' or 'even' (see translation in note above).

mobilitate . . . an ne altius scrutaretur – 'because of the fickleness ... or perhaps to avoid investigating it too deeply'. Note the *variatio*, as the purpose clause is contrasted with the causal ablative *mobilitate*.

quoquo modo acta – 'the deeds, in whatever way (they had been done)', object of *comprobasse*.

comprobasse – shortened version of *comprobavisse*. Syncopated forms dropping -*vi*- are common in Tacitus.

accepta – supply *est*.

inviso ... adferebant – 'once the *princeps* had become hated, his deeds whether good or bad brought him equal unpopularity'.

7.3

venalia cuncta – supply *erant* here and with the following adjectives. The archaic *cuncta* (instead of *omnia*) elevates the diction.

subitis – 'in the unexpected circumstances'.

tamquam apud senem festinantes – 'in a hurry as happens under an old master'. The slaves are rushing to make as much profit as they can before Galba dies. There is *variatio* in the use of the adjective *avidae* and the participle *festinantes*. The two words really refer to the slaves, but agree with *manus*. This transferral of adjective is a device known as *hypallage*.

eademque novae aulae mala – i.e. the same as in Nero's court. *aula* is a loaded term, used by other authors of eastern rulers and mythological kings, but for the first time of Roman rulers by Tacitus.

non aeque excusata – because Nero was young and charismatic.

inrisui ac fastidio erat – predicative datives (*Oxford Latin Grammar*, pp. 12–13): 'was a source of mockery and disgust'.

adsuetis iuventae Neronis – 'for those accustomed to Nero's youth'. Nero was only thirty when he died.

forma ac decore corporis – ablatives of respect (see n. 6.2 *introitus*): 'in their appearance and physical grace'.

Chapters 8–11: Tacitus now considers the state of affairs outside Rome. Most worrying are the feelings amongst the German legions, who are described as anxious and angry. Tacitus also names the future emperors Vitellius, who Galba has sent to command the disaffected troops in Lower Germany, and Vespasian, who is fighting a war against the Jews. He ends by darkly foreshadowing the death of Galba and the near destruction of the Roman state.

After surveying the empire, Tacitus begins the narrative proper with an account of Galba's deeds in Rome (Chapters 12–20), focusing on his adoption of Piso.

AS

Chapter 12

12.1

paucis post kalendas Ianuarias diebus – 'a few days after the first of January'. Roman dates are counted in relation to one of three key days: the Kalends (1st of every month), the Nones (5th of most months but 7th of March, May, July and October) and the Ides (13th of most months but 15th of March, May, July and October). It is also worth noting that the Romans counted back from these dates inclusively. For more on dates see *Oxford Latin Grammar*, pp. 145–146. *paucis ... diebus* is ablative of measure of difference ('after ... *by* a few days').

Pompei Propinqui procuratoris – for the role of *procurator* see n. 7.1 *Trebonius*. This individual is mentioned only here and at *Histories* 1.58 where he is put to death by Vitellius.

Belgica – *Gallia Belgica* (Belgic Gaul) was a province centred on Belgium and northern France.

adferuntur – historic present.

superioris Germaniae – the province of Upper Germany lay upstream (south) of Lower Germany (*Germania Inferior*) along the Rhine, over parts of France, Switzerland and Germany.

legiones ... flagitare et ... permittere – accusative and infinitive to report the content of the letters ('saying that ...'). *legiones* is the subject of both infinitives.

rupta ... reverentia – an ablative absolute, while *sacramenti* is objective genitive (see n. 5.1 *Caesarum*). The fact it is not the oath itself that is broken, but the abstract noun *reverentia*, makes the rebellion seem like a more general collapse of morality.

AS

eligendi – 'of choosing', a gerund (see *Oxford Latin Grammar*, pp. 108–109).

quo seditio mollius acciperetur – 'so that the revolt might be received more leniently'. *quo* is used instead of *ut* when a purpose clause contains a comparative (literally 'by which the more . . .').

12.2

maturavit – 'brought to fruition' or 'hastened'; the metaphor is of crops ripening. Note the emphatic position.

proximis – used here as a noun: 'intimates' or 'associates'.

tota civitate – 'in the whole state' – 'place where' expressions do not need a preposition when they contain the adjective *totus* (or *medius*).

sermo – 'topic of conversation'.

licentia ac libidine . . . aetate – 'because of . . .', three causal ablatives. *licentia* refers to the freedom to talk, and *libido* to the enjoyment of exercising it. *loquendi* is a gerund (see *eligendi* above).

fessa – the use of *fessus* with an abstract noun ('tired' or 'feeble old age') is poetic.

12.3

paucis – supply *erat*. Literally 'there was to few', and therefore 'few had'.

iudicium – 'sound judgement'.

prout quis amicus vel cliens, hunc vel illum . . . destinabant – 'marked out this man or that, depending on to whom he was a friend or client'. *quis* may be taken as an archaic form of *quibus*, and *erat* should be supplied in the clause. For *cliens* see n. 4.3 *clientes*.

AS

in Titi Vinii odium – 'for the sake of their hatred for . . .'. There is *variatio* as the preposition phrase is correlated with the causal ablative *stulta spe* ('out of foolish hope'). *Titi Vinii* is objective genitive.

in dies – 'every day'.

quanto potentior eodem actu invisior erat – 'became more hated with the same momentum with which he became more unpopular', with *erat* supplied after *quanto*. Tacitus is varying the common construction *quanto . . . tanto* ('the more . . . the more . .', ablatives of measure of difference).

hiantes . . . cupiditates – 'open-mouthed greed', a particularly poetic phrase. The word *hio* ('gape', 'be open mouthed') really refers to Galba's friends who are eager for imperial favours, but agrees with the abstract noun *cupiditates*, another example of *hypallage* (see n. 7.3 *tamquam*).

cum . . . peccaretur – another distinctive feature of Tacitus' style is his fondness for ending a sentence or chapter with a pithy, neatly expressed statement (an 'epigram'). When these express a more general truth that can be detached from the context, they are known as *sententiae*. They elevate the narrative and exhibit Tacitus' keen understanding of human psychology, often with an unsettling effect.

peccaretur – impersonal passive. Literally 'it might be sinned', but better in English as 'sins might be committed'. It is a powerful verb form as its subject is effectively the action itself. Here the lack of the personal subject also has a generalizing effect, emphasizing Galba's lack of control.

AS

Chapter 13

13.1

principatus – genitive singular (fourth declension).

divisa in . . . – supply *est* and translate *in* as 'between' here. There is asyndeton between *consulem* and *Cornelium*.

nec minor gratia Icelo – *gratia* here means 'influence' and *erat* should be supplied (for *esse* + dative, see n. 12.3 *paucis*). Galba's freedman Icelus had been imprisoned by Nero in Rome, but upon Nero's suicide he travelled to Spain in only seven days to inform Galba.

anulis donatum – 'presented with (golden) rings'. Slaves wore iron rings to show their status, but equestrians (see n. 4.3 *primores*) had the right to wear gold rings. Someone could usually only attain equestrian status if they passed the wealth threshold, were born free, and had a free father and grandfather. This is overlooked in the case of Icelus.

vocitabant – the subject is an unspecified 'they' ('people') and the suffix *-ito* gives the verb frequentative meaning: 'people often called him'.

rebus minoribus – 'in less important matters'.

sibi quisque tendentes – 'each straining for his own ends'. *quisque* refers to each member of a plurality individually, and is therefore often found in the singular but agreeing with plurals.

circa – 'with regard to'.

eligendi successoris – 'of choosing a successor'. When a gerund takes an object, a gerundive agreeing with the noun is used instead (i.e. not *eligendi successorem*), a process called gerundival attraction (see *Oxford Latin Grammar*, pp. 108–109).

AS

13.2

M. Othone – this is the first mention of Otho, who later becomes emperor after overthrowing Galba. Tacitus describes his character and background in detail later in this chapter, and in Chapters 21–23.

non tam ... quam – 'not so much ... as'.

unum aliquem – 'any individual' (see also Chapter 6). What binds them is opposition to Otho, rather than support of anyone in particular.

rumoribus ... transmittentium – 'in the gossip of those who pass over ...'.

quia Vinio vidua filia, caelebs Otho – there is *asyndeton* here, and *erat* should be supplied in each phrase (see n. 12.3 *paucis* for *erat* + dative).

subisse – supply *Galbam*.

translatae – 'since it would have been removed', agreeing with *rei publicae*. The participle functions as the apodosis to the conditional which follows.

si ... relinqueretur – 'if it were to be left'. Since this reports Galba's thoughts, it functions as a suboblique clause (see n. 7.2 *postquam*), becoming subjunctive and following the rules for the sequence of tenses. The imperfect subjunctive (most likely) represents a present subjunctive in direct speech (the protasis of a remote future conditional; see *Oxford Latin Grammar*, pp. 114–17).

13.3

aemulatione – causal ablative ('because of ...').

eo – 'for this reason'. The subject of this sentence, and the one that follows, is Nero.

AS

Poppaeam Sabinam – the details surrounding Poppaea are hazy. Here she is described as being Nero's courtesan before she started an affair with Otho which caused Nero to send him away. A different version of the story is given in *Annals* 13.45–46, in which she was initially the wife of the praetorian prefect Rufrius Crispinus, and then married Otho after having an affair. While married to Otho she became Nero's mistress, so he sent Otho to Lusitania. Further contrasting versions of this story are also given by Plutarch, Suetonius and Cassius Dio. She is also said to have encouraged Nero to kill his mother Agrippina and his wife Octavia, before being killed while pregnant by a kick from her new husband. After her death she was deified by Nero.

principale scortum – after the elevating adjective *principale*, the harsh, colloquial word *scortum* ('whore') is particularly jarring. Its literal meaning is 'skin', and its neuter gender adds to the depersonalizing and objectifying power of the word.

ut apud conscium libidinum – 'as (was natural) into the keeping of one who was aware of his passions'.

donec . . . amoliretur – 'until he could get rid of . . .'. The subjunctive is used in temporal clauses when there is more than just a temporal connection between clauses, here that of purpose (see *Oxford Latin Grammar*, pp. 118–121).

in eadem Poppaea – translate *in* as 'in relation to'.

Lusitaniam – province covering modern Portugal and parts of Spain. Otho was governor here from AD 58–68.

specie legationis – translate *specie* as 'pretext'. Normally someone would have held a praetorship before becoming a governor, but Otho had only been a quaestor.

AS

13.4

in partes transgressus – *pars* is often used in the plural by Tacitus when it means 'faction'; here understand *Galbae*.

nec segnis – the understatement using a negative serves to emphasize the meaning (*litotes*).

similem – i.e. to Nero. The appendix structure of the sentence (two ablative absolutes after the main verb) places this scathing statement in the emphatic final position.

Chapter 14

14.1

nihil . . . certum – supply *erat*.

Vitellio – the Upper German legions had refused to swear allegiance to Galba on 1 January, and sided with Vitellius on 3 January. Tacitus passes over the details here, but he picks up the narrative at Chapter 50, and Vitellius remains a focus until his death at the end of Book III.

anxius quonam . . . erumperet – the construction here is unusual. While *quonam* introduces an indirect question, *erumperet* is imperfect subjunctive as is normal when clauses dependent on words of fearing (*anxius*) refer to the future (*Oxford Latin Grammar*, pp. 102–103): 'anxious as to how far exactly the violence of the armies would break out'. The suffix *-nam* emphasizes the interrogative, highlighting Galba's anxiety.

confisus – *confido* is semi-deponent.

quod . . . rebatur – refers to the whole of the main clause that follows. It is best left until afterwards in translation: 'which he thought was . . .'.

AS

comitia imperii transigit – 'he conducted an imperial election'. This is a striking phrase: *comitia* usually refers to an assembly of the Roman people for electing important magistrates such as consuls, a practice that had ceased in the Principate. The use of the word to describe a meeting of only five men, to announce the adoption that Galba has already decided upon, is heavily ironic. *transigit* (and *iubet* later) is historic present.

Mario Celso – consul-elect noted for his loyalty as he served under Nero, Galba, Otho, Vitellius and Vespasian in a number of military and political roles. For his survival of Otho's rebellion see Chapter 45.

Ducenio Gemino praefecto urbis – the city prefect was appointed to maintain order in Rome and its surrounding area, and had charge of the urban cohorts (see n. 4.2 *urbanum*).

Pisonem Licinianum – Galba's choice of successor was a young nobleman exiled by Nero. There is a short obituary at Chapter 48.

accersiri – both *accersi* and *accersiri* are found as the present passive infinitive.

propria electione – causal ablative. Translate as 'because it was his own choice'.

cui ... exercita ... amicitia – 'who had a friendship ... which had been cultivated', another example of the dative + 'to be' (supply *erat*). Some commentators take *cui* as dative of agent ('by') but the difference is subtle. *exercita* is perfect passive participle from *exerceo*.

Rubellium Plautum – a wealthy great-grandson of Tiberius, executed by a paranoid Nero in AD 62.

ut ignotum – 'as if he were a stranger'.

AS

de Pisone – translate as 'Piso's'. There is a sign here of how the genitive came to be replaced by words such as *de* and *di* in Romance languages.

fidem – 'credibility'.

14.2

M. Crasso et Scribonia genitus – *genitus* ('born from' or 'the son of') takes the ablative. Piso's father had been consul in AD 27, and was descended from the famous Republican figure M. Licinius Crassus, while Scribonia was a descendant of Pompey the Great.

vultu habituque – ablatives of respect ('in . . .').

moris antiqui ... severus – *variatio* (genitive of description + adjective).

deterius interpretantibus – 'by those who interpreted things less favourably'. *interpretantibus* is a dative of agent, and there is *variatio* with the earlier ablative *aestimatione recta*.

tristior habebatur – 'was considered rather ill-humoured'.

ea ... placebat – 'the more that part of his character was viewed as suspicious by anxious men, the more it was pleasing to the one who was adopting him'. *quo ... eo* is often used with comparatives (like *quanto ... tanto*, see n. 12.3 *quanto*) to mean 'the more x ... the more y'. Here Tacitus has omitted the corresponding *eo* and the second comparative. *erat* should be supplied with *suspectior*, and the contrast is emphasized by the juxtaposition of *sollicitis adoptanti*.

Chapters 15–16: After taking Piso by the hand, Galba addresses him in direct speech. This marks the adoption of Piso, but Galba also justifies adoption as a mode of succession, praises Piso's qualities and advises him on how to govern. The very personal and private nature of the first speech in the Histories *is notably different from the grand, public set speeches that are common in historians of earlier periods.*

AS

Chapter 17

17.1

ferunt – 'people say', introducing an accusative and infinitive (*Pisonem
. . . prodidisse*). Leave the words *statim . . . oculis* till last in translation.

statim intuentibus – 'to those looking on immediately', dative
after *prodidisse,* and meaning those who were present at the private
comitia.

mox coniectis . . . . oculis – ablative absolute (*variatio* after the dative
intuentibus) referring to Piso's later appearances in public.

nullum . . . motum – best taken as 'any sign'.

reverens – supply *erat.*

de se – usually the reflexive *se* refers back to the grammatical subject
(*sermo*), but here it refers to Piso who is the subject in sense ('about
himself').

mutatum – supply *est.*

quasi – 'as if', but may be translated here as 'he looked like one who
was . . .'. The subjunctive after *quasi* follows the usual rules for the
sequence of tenses.

17.2

consultatum – 'a discussion was held', impersonal passive with *est*
omitted (see n. 12.3 *peccaretur*).

pro rostris . . . adoptio noncuparetur – 'as to whether the adoption
should be proclaimed from the *rostra*'. An indirect question, with
utrum to be supplied. The word *noncuparetur* is best taken as a
deliberative question ('should?'), which would also be subjunctive in
direct speech. The *rostra* was a platform in the Forum from which

AS

orations and announcements were made to the public. *pro* means 'on the front of' but is best rendered as 'from' here.

castris – the praetorian camp, just outside the walls on the north-east of the city.

iri . . . placuit – 'it was decided to go', literally 'to be gone' (impersonal passive). The lack of defined subjects (as *consultatum* above) make the decision-making seem hasty and confused.

honorificum . . . fore – '(they thought) that this would be a mark of honour'. In Latin the shift to accusative and infinitive is enough to signal an indirect statement, but in English words such as 'they thought' often have to be supplied. *fore* is another form of *futurum esse*, the future infinitive of *sum*.

quorum . . . spernendum – a tricky section. The accusative and infinitive construction continues after *quorum*, as here it is a connective ('and their'), and not introducing a relative clause ('whose') which would require a subjunctive verb (it would be suboblique). *ut . . . ita* again means 'although . . . nevertheless' (see n. 4.2 *ut*), while *esse* should be supplied with *spernendum,* a gerundive of obligation (*Oxford Latin Grammar*, pp. 111–112). *male* has a definite moral sense here, unlike the English 'badly' which means 'not well'. Translate as 'and that although it was wrong for their (i.e. the soldiers') favour to be acquired through bribery and corruption, nevertheless it should not be scorned (when it was acquired) through good practices'.

circumsteterat . . . . publica expectatio – may be translated as 'an expectant crowd', but this use of an abstract noun ('the expectation of the people') as the subject of such a concrete verb ('had surrounded') is a striking example of personification. The effect is to widen the scope from the particular crowd to a general sense of the forces at work and the pressures on Galba. Further emphasis is provided by the inverted word order and the tense of the verb (pluperfect for already completed action). Tacitus may be encouraging us to reflect on whether Galba's decision to announce the adoption to the troops first was the correct one.

Palatium – 'the Palatine hill' which overlooked the Forum, or 'the palace' which was built on it (from which the English word comes).

impatiens – 'impatient (to hear)', followed by the genitive.

male coercitam – 'badly concealed' (unlike earlier use of *male*).

supprimentes – 'those who tried to suppress'.

Chapter 18

18.1

quartum idus Ianuarias – 'the tenth of January'. With *diem ante* supplied, literally 'the fourth day before the Ides of January' (by inclusive counting). For Roman dates see n. 12.1 *paucis*.

observatum id antiquitus comitiis dirimendis – 'the observation of this, which traditionally caused the breaking up of assemblies'. *observatum*, although a participle, holds the primary meaning and is best translated as an abstract noun. This idiom is also seen in the title of Livy's history, *ab urbe condita* ('from the founding of the city'). *antiquitus* is an adverb, and *comitiis diremendis* is a dative gerundive expressing purpose (see n. 6.2 *opprimendis*), although here closer to the idea of 'causing'.

terruit . . . quo minus – 'scare away from'. For *quo minus* + subjunctive with verbs of prevention see *Oxford Latin Grammar*, pp.131–132.

contemptorem – typically Tacitean *brevitas*. The noun provides an explanation for Galba's actions, answered by the alternative reason introduced by *seu*. Translate as 'either because he despised'.

AS

ut – 'on the grounds that they were'.

seu – 'or because'.

quae fato manent – supply *ea* as the antecedent of *quae*: 'things which are fixed by fate'.

non vitantur – '(cannot) be avoided'.

18.2

imperatoria brevitate – 'with the brevity befitting an emperor'. Compare this with the extended direct speech at the private meeting.

quo ... legeret – suboblique subjunctive. This refers to the ancient Italian practice of levying troops by which the first soldier selected a recruit, who then made the next selection, and so on. This process continued until the required number was reached. Galba is trying to tailor his speech to the military audience, and to give legitimacy to his decision by evoking the past.

pronuntiat – historic present (also *adseverat, addit, respondent*).

dissimulata – 'because it had been concealed'.

in maius crederetur – 'be believed to be greater (than it was)'. *maius* is the comparative neuter adjective of *magnus*.

ultro – see n. 7.2 *ultro*.

quartam et duoetvicensimam legiones – both stationed at Moguntiacum (modern-day Mainz) in Upper Germany. These were the legions that first revolted against Galba on 1 January (see Chapter 55).

errasse – syncopated form of *erravisse*.

brevi – 'soon', short for *in brevi tempore*.

AS

in officio fore – translate as 'would return to duty'. For *fore* see n. 17.2 *honorificum.*

aut pretium – note the emphatic position, which highlights Galba's refusal to provide a donative.

18.3

tribuni . . . centurionesque – officers within the Praetorian Guard. At the time of Galba the Praetorian Guard probably consisted of twelve cohorts of 500 (possibly 1000) men, each of which was commanded by a military tribune. The cohorts were further divided into centuries, units of around 100 men, each led by a centurion. The officers were more loyal to Galba as they would have been confirmed in their positions after he became emperor.

grata auditu – 'things pleasing to hear'. *auditu* is a form known as the supine, from *audio.* It declines like a fourth declension noun, but is found solely in the accusative and ablative. In the latter (as here) it only appears with adjectives and some nouns (e.g. *fas, nefas*) as an ablative of respect or specification. Compare also the Latin phrase, sometimes found in English, *mirabile dictu* – 'wonderful to say'.

maestitia ac silentium – supply *erat.*

tamquam – 'on the grounds that' + subjunctive (usual rules of sequence).

donativi necessitatem – 'their claim to a donative'. *necessitatem* denotes that there was an obligation on the part of the emperor to provide this.

bello – the soldiers had received donatives from Claudius when he adopted Nero, and from Nero upon his accession (*in pace*). They are angry because their real efforts in the fighting to depose Nero (*bello*) had not been rewarded by Galba.

nocuit – supply *ei* ('him').

cui iam pares non sumus – '(qualities) to which we no longer measure up'. See Chapter 5 for more evidence of Galba being out of step with the times (and particularly n. 5.2 *nec*).

Chapter 19

19.1

non comptior – *sermo* is the subject, and *erat* should be supplied (and again with *oratio*).

sermo . . . oratio – careful use of vocabulary here: an *oratio* is more formal and polished than a *sermo*.

multi – supply *favebant* with each subject in this sentence. Tacitus now undercuts the simple description of support (*et . . . aderat*) with the motivations behind it for three different sections of the senate. Things are not as simple as they appear on the surface.

effusius qui noluerant – supply *ei* as the antecedent of *qui*: '(those) who had not wanted (the adoption gave their support) more effusively'.

medii ac plurimi – *ac* is here explanatory, not introducing a new group, but further defining *medii*: 'the indifferent, who were the majority'.

sequenti quadriduo – ablative of time within which. The adoption was on 10 January, and the murder on 15 January.

quod medium inter . . . fuit – 'which intervened between'.

dictum . . . factumve – supply *est*.

19.2

crebrioribus . . . nuntiis – ablative absolute with verb understood: 'since messages (were becoming) more frequent'.

AS

ad accipienda credendaque omnia – gerundival attraction (see n. 13.1 *eligendi*)

omnia nova cum tristia sunt – 'all news when it is bad'. *cum* meaning 'when' takes the indicative in primary sequence. The ablative absolute *facili civitate* should therefore be taken as a general statement about the Roman people ('as the citizens are always ready . . .').

mittendos – gerundive of obligation, supply *esse*.

agitatum – impersonal passive, supply *est*.

et – 'also' (here and in the next sentence).

num . . . proficisceretur – deliberative indirect question (see n. 17.2 *pro*).

maiore praetextu . . . laturus – literally 'so that with greater display they would bring . . . and he would bring' but the real emphasis is on *maiore praetextu* so 'which would be a greater display, as they would bring . . .' works better in translation. *laturus* describes both *illi* and *hic*, but agrees grammatically with the nearer word as is common in Latin. *illi* refers to the senators who made up the rest of the delegation, and is nominative because their presence is implied in the earlier *et* ('also').

nominati, excusati, substituti – supply *sunt*. The asyndeton emphasizes Galba's acquiescence and indecisiveness.

ambitu remanendi aut eundi – 'because of their manoeuvring to remain or to go'. *ambitu* is a causal ablative and *remanendi* and *eundi* are gerunds (n. 12.1 *eligendi*).

ut – 'depending on how'.

Chapter 20

20.1

cura – supply *erat*.

cuncta scrutantibus – 'to those examining everything'.

inde repeti ubi . . . – '(for money) to be sought from the place where . . .'. *pecuniam* is the implied subject of *repeti*.

bis et viciens miliens sestertium – '22 hundred million sesterces' (22 x 1,000 x 100,000). For an idea of the value of this see n. 5.1 *donativum*.

donationibus – 'in gifts'.

appellari – 'to be called to pay back the money'.

iussit – i.e. Galba.

decima parte – 'a tenth', the usual way to denote fractions. *decimae portiones* (literally 'one-tenth shares') may also be translated in the same way.

super . . . erant – *supererant*. This splitting up of a word is called *tmesis*. It also happens sometimes in English, e.g. 'a-whole-nother thing'.

isdem erga aliena sumptibus quibus – literally 'because of the same extravagances with respect to (the money) of others with which . . .'. Better in English as its own clause: 'because they had extravagantly spent the money of others in the same way as . . .'. *aliena* refers to the money which was unfairly confiscated by Nero and given to them, so not theirs to waste.

rapacissimo cuique ac perditissimo – the superlative with *quisque* means 'all the most x . . .'. This is a dative of possession, so 'of all the most greedy and depraved men'.

AS

instrumenta vitiorum – Tacitus is purposefully vague, allowing our imagination to fill in the details.

20.2

praepositi – supply *sunt*.

novum...genus – nominative, loosely in apposition (noun describing a noun) to the officials.

ambitu ac numero onerosum – there is some ambiguity here. Is it onerous for the state or the officials? *ambitu* could refer to the corrupt actions of people who wanted a place on the board, or of those wishing to pay back less than required. Furthermore *numero* may denote the number of officials, or the number of people who had to pay back money. Perhaps the answer is a mixture of all the above, so retain the ambiguity in translation: 'onerous because of corruption and the numbers involved'.

hasta et sector – supply *erat* here and with *urbs*. A spear was stuck in the ground to indicate that an auction was taking place as it was originally the sign of plunder taken in war, while a *sector* was someone who bought confiscated property at auction in order to make a profit by reselling it. Translate as 'auctions and speculators'.

ac tamen – 'and yet'.

gaudium – supply *erat*.

quod ... forent – 'on the grounds that ... would be ...'. *quod* + subjunctive gives an alleged reason (*Oxford Latin Grammar*, pp. 126–127) while *forent* is another form for *essent*.

quibus ... quibus – 'those to whom ... those from whom ...'. Supply *ei* both times. The second is a dative of disadvantage, meaning 'from' with verbs of removal or taking away.

AS

donasset – syncopated form of *donavisset*, 'had granted (gifts)'.

20.3

exauctorati ... tribuni – supply *sunt* and for *tribuni* see n. 18.3 *tribuni*. The reasons behind this are not given but it was probably for involvement with Nymphidius Sabinus.

urbanis cohortibus – see n. 4.2 *urbanum*.

Aemilius Pacensis – he and Fronto were later generals under Otho. Little else is known about these four men.

vigilibus – the *vigiles* acted as the city's night watch and fire service (different from the urban cohorts mentioned above).

in ceteros – 'against the rest'.

metus initium – repeat *fuit*.

tamquam – 'on the grounds that' (n. 18.3 *tamquam*) or 'as they believed that'.

per artem et formidine – 'cunningly and through fear', more *variatio*.

Chapters 21–26 explain the circumstances that led to Otho's rebellion.

Chapter 21

21.1

compositis rebus – 'in peaceful conditions'.

cui ... nulla spes – dative + *sum* (*erat* supplied): 'who had no hope'.

omne in turbido consilium – '(and) whose whole purpose depended on a turbulent situation'. *cui* and *erat* to be supplied.

AS

luxuria . . . inopia . . . ira . . . invidia – nominatives in apposition to *multa*.

onerosa – 'which would have been burdensome'.

toleranda – gerundive, 'which could have been tolerated'.

et – 'also'.

quo magis concupisceret – purpose clause (see n. 12.1 *quo*): 'so that he could be more desirous' or even 'so that he could give freer rein to his desires'. Otho convinces himself that he is in danger so that he might not feel guilty about his ambitions for power.

praegravem . . . perire – the syntax shifts into indirect speech until the end of the chapter. All main verbs become accusative and infinitive, and verbs in subordinate clauses are subjunctive. In English supply 'he said that' (see n. 17.2 *honorificum*).

Lusitaniam – see n. 13.3 *Lusitaniam*.

honorem – heavily sarcastic.

expectandum – gerundive of obligation, supply *esse*. Take with both *Lusitaniam* and *honorem* (for its agreement with *honorem* see n. 19.2 *maiore*).

suspectum . . . invisumque – supply *esse*. The subject is *eum* to be supplied before *qui* (see following note).

qui proximus destinaretur – 'that he who was marked out as next (in line)', i.e. by public opinion.

nociturum – supply *esse*.

occidi Othonem posse – Otho refers to himself in the third person, either to make his statement more emphatic or to mean 'an Otho' or 'someone like Otho'.

AS

21.2

agendum audendumque – supply *esse*. An impersonal use of the gerundive (*Oxford Latin Grammar*, p. 112): 'it should be done and dared', so 'he should act and be daring'.

fluxa – supply *esset*.

Pisonis – repeat *auctoritas*.

transitus rerum – literally 'changes of situations', or 'times of transition'. Supply *esse*.

opus – *opus est* + ablative = 'there is need of . . .'. Here supply *esse*.

sit . . . maneat – *repraesentatio* (see n. 7.2 *postquam*).

mortem . . . distingui – literally 'that death (which was) equal to all according to nature was distinguished by oblivion or glory among future generations'. In English it is better separated into two clauses, i.e. 'that death naturally affected all, but each man's death was marked out either as worthy of forgetting or worthy of glory among future generations'.

acrioris viri esse – 'it was (the duty) of a more vigorous man'.

merito – 'deservingly' or 'for a purpose'.

Chapter 22

22.1

et corpori similis – *et* here is explanatory ('that is to say', for *ac* used similarly see n. 19.1 *medii*). Best left out in translation.

et . . . retinebitur – a particularly long and involved sentence (mapped out below). The complex syntax is indicative of the many voices and opinions coming to bear on Otho.

AS

The first half (*et ... exprobrabant*) concerns Otho's closest slaves and freedmen. The subject comes first (*et ... servorumque)*, then a participle phrase (*corruptius ... habiti*); there is then a string of accusatives (*aulam ... libidines*) that should be taken with another nominative participle (*ostentates*) and a short conditional (*si auderet*) thrown in for good measure. Finally comes the bulk of the main clause (*quiescenti ... exprobrabant*).

The second half of the sentence is a long appendix after the main verb, relating to his astrologers (*urgentibus ... retinebitur*). It begins with an ablative absolute (*urgentibus ... mathematicis*), followed by a temporal clause (*dum ... adfirmant*), a description in apposition to the subject of the *dum* clause (*genus ... fallax*) and a relative clause (*quod ... retinebitur*).

quam in privata domo – 'than (is usual) in a private household'. The point is that the slaves of the most powerful were usually the most immoral, but Otho's slaves are behaving badly even before he has official power.

regnorum – treat as singular: 'the vices of royal power'. The word *regnorum* is a strong choice of vocabulary. In its early days Rome had been ruled by kings, an institution abolished after the deposition of Tarquin the Proud. In the Republican period many were fiercely opposed to the idea of monarchical rule and the early emperors were keen to convey the idea that they were not absolute monarchs, but merely the *Princeps* ('first citizen') or the *primus inter pares* ('first among equals').

aulam ... exprobrabant – '(spoke) to him, eager for such things, about Nero's court ... and held out the prospect (of these pleasures) as his own if he was daring, but reproached him as they would be another's since he was being inactive'. Translation of this tricky section has been aided by adding a verb of saying and treating *ostentates* as a main verb.

si auderet – technically a suboblique subjunctive as Tacitus is

AS

reporting the words of the slaves and freedmen (represents future indicative of direct speech).

si auderet ... quiescenti – a nuanced example of *variatio*, as the participle suggests the actual state of things, to show how the slaves and freedmen are trying to shame Otho into action.

exprobrabant – ironically suggests they are concerned with his moral integrity.

urgentibus etiam mathematicis – best to take as the main clause of a new sentence in translation.

dum ... adfirmant – 'declaring' ('while' is awkward here in English).

novos motus – 'revolution' (like *res novae*), although some translators take as 'strange movements (of the stars)'.

clarum – clever choice of word, capturing the ambiguity of this kind of prophecy. Otho takes it to mean 'glorious', but 'famous' is equally apt as he eventually commits suicide after only three months as emperor.

genus ... infidum ... fallax – nominative describing the astrologers (see syntax breakdown above).

quod ... retinebitur – this chapter contains a particularly large number of *sententiae* (see n. 12.3 *cum*). Astrologers had been expelled from Rome by Augustus, Tiberius and Claudius, but no measures were conclusive and they continued to be consulted, even by emperors themselves.

22.2

secreta Poppaeae ... habuerant – 'Poppaea's secret dealings had employed', but some take *secreta* to mean 'hidden rooms'. For Poppaea see n. 13.3 *Poppaeam*.

AS

pessimum ... instrumentum – in apposition to *mathematicos*. Translate as 'the most wicked tools for the wife of an emperor', but it may also imply that she used her astrologers to secure the marriage in the first place ('for (gaining) a marriage with an emperor').

e quibus – connecting relative ('from them').

superfuturum – supply *esse*.

postquam ex eventu fides – supply a verb, e.g. 'after (he had won) credibility from the occurrence (of this)'. *eventu* refers to the death of Nero which he had predicted.

rumore ... computantium – 'with the gossip of those who compared ...'. *senium* here is 'old age' (as n. 5.2 *senium*).

fore ut ... adscisceretur – literally 'that it would be the case that he would be adopted', and therefore 'that he would be adopted'. *fore ut* + subjunctive is often used instead of the (rare) future passive infinitive (see *Oxford Latin Grammar*, p. 83).

22.3

cupidine ingenii humani ... credendi – 'because of the desire in human nature of believing ...'. *cupidine* is ablative of cause and *credo* may take the accusative when it means 'accept as true'.

et – 'even' or 'also'.

sceleris instinctor – another example of Tacitus' predilection for nouns, which are often best translated as verbs in English: 'was urging him (to commit) crime'.

ad quod facillime ... transitur – literally 'to which it is crossed very easily from', so 'a step which is very easily taken'. The antecedent of *quod* is *sceleris*, and *transitur* is impersonal passive.

ab eius modi voto – prepositions may be separated from the word they govern by words which go closely with that word (commonly, as here, a genitive).

Chapter 23

23.1

incertum – 'it is doubtful', supply *est*.

an repens – supply *fuerit* (subject is the promoted *cogitatio*).

adfectaverat – Otho is the subject.

spe . . . paratu – ablatives of cause.

itinere – the journey from Spain with Galba.

vetustissimum quemque – see n. 20.1 *rapacissimo*. Due to his exile in Lusitania, Otho only knows the older soldiers.

memoria . . . appellando – 'calling them messmates because of the memory of their service to Nero', reminding us of Otho's connection with Nero. Take the ablative gerund *appellando* (and *inserendo* later) as equivalent to the present participle. In Romance languages this gerund takes over the role of the participle (e.g. Italian *crescendo/diminuendo*) and the beginning of the process is evident here.

agnoscere . . . requirere . . . iuvare – historic infinitives, which should be translated as main verbs with Otho as subject. These add pace and vividness because all focus is on the action, with no reference to time or agency.

saepius – 'rather often', as often when comparatives are used without a comparison.

AS

quaeque alia turbamenta vulgi – i.e. *et alia quae turbamenta vulgi erant*.

23.2

duritia imperii – 'harshness of discipline'.

Campaniae lacus et Achaiae urbes – *Campania* is a region of Italy and *Achaia* is the name of the Roman province of Greece. There may be an error from Tacitus here because these were trips made by praetorians accompanying Nero, but there is no mention elsewhere of praetorians marching from Spain to Rome with Galba. *Neroniani comitatus* above also implies that Tacitus is talking about the Praetorian Guard.

Chapters 24–25: Tacitus relates some instances of Otho's bribery of the praetorians. Otho then entrusts the plot to his freedman Onomastus, who uses two members of the guard to stir up the soldiers' anxieties.

Chapter 26

26.1

infecit ea tabes – a strong metaphor. The *tabes* ('disease') is the growing spirit of mutiny.

legionum . . . auxiliorum – the regular troops stationed in Rome and listed in 6.2.

postquam vulgatum erat – the pluperfect (rather than the perfect) with *postquam* is usually only used in Classical Latin when the interval of time is stated (e.g. 'two days after . . .').

adeo . . . destinaretur – a difficult sentence. First comes the main clause(s) (*adeo . . . fuit*), followed by a result clause (*ut . . . fuerint*) and a conditional (*ni . . . timuissent*). Then there is a causal ablative (*cura*), a relative clause (*quam ... parabant*) and a fear clause (*sed ne ... destinaretur*) which contains an *ut*-clause. Again, the complexity of the syntax reflects the confusion of the soldiers and the aborted attempt.

adeoque parata apud .....dissimulatio fuit – literally 'and so ready was the revolt among the bad (soldiers), (and) even pretended ignorance among the honest' but better as 'so ready were the bad soldiers for revolt and even the honest to feign ignorance of it'.

integros – denotes moral integrity, while subtly continuing the disease metaphor ('untainted', 'healthy').

postero iduum die – 'the fourteenth of January' ('the day after the Ides').

rapturi fuerint, ni . . . timuissent – 'they would have seized ... if they had not been afraid of ...'. The unusual form *rapturi fuerint* is used because it is both the main clause of an unfulfilled past conditional, and further subordinated in a result clause. They were going to seize him to take him to the praetorian camp and declare him emperor.

incerta noctis – 'uncertainties of the night'.

tota urbe – see n. 12.2 *tota*.

nec facilem inter temulentos consensum – literally 'and the not easy collective action among drunk men' or 'and the difficulty of collective action when men are drunk'.

quam – antecedent is *rei publicae*.

sobrii – 'when they were sober'.

sed ne . . . pro Othone destinaretur – fear clause following on from *timuissent*: 'but (out of fear) that ... would be mistaken for Otho' (and proclaimed emperor).

AS

ut quisque ... – 'whenever anyone' or simply 'whoever'.

oblatus esset – suboblique subjunctive as this reports the fear in the minds of the soldiers. The passive of *offero* is used with the dative in the sense of 'encounter' or 'come upon'.

Pannonici – see n. 6.2 *Illyrico*.

militibus ... ignorantibus plerisque – as foreign auxiliaries, they were unacquainted with Otho and his appearance.

26.2

per – 'by'.

oppressa – supply *sunt*.

apud Galbae aures – 'in Galba's hearing', literally 'in the presence of Galba's ears'.

ignarus – according to Suetonius (*Galba* 14) Laco was a judge's assistant before prefect and had never been a soldier. Tacitus lays on three adjectives, coming emphatically after the main verb, to describe his incompetence.

consilii – take with *inimicus* (see following note).

quod ... adferret – generic subjunctive (see n. 7.2 *fuere*), so 'hostile to *any* plan which ...'.

The second half of the selection describes the actual day of the revolt. Chapters 27–35 narrate the initial stages, beginning with Otho slipping away while Galba is performing a sacrifice. News is brought of the revolt and measures are taken by Galba. A false rumour arrives, claiming that Otho has been killed, and Galba finally leaves the palace.

AS

Chapter 27

27.1

octavo decimo kalendas Februarias – 'on the fifteenth of January'. Literally 'on the eighteenth (day before) the Kalends of February', with *die ante* supplied and working on the Roman method of inclusive counting (see n. 12.1 *paucis*).

aede Apollinis – situated on the Palatine Hill (see n. 17.2 *Palatium*).

haruspex – a soothsayer who foretold events by inspection of sacrificial entrails, a practice that came from the Etruscans.

tristia – 'unfavourable'.

praedicit – Tacitus adds to the excitement by using the historic present in this section.

audiente Othone . . . – Tacitus uses an appendix to move focus onto the superstitious Otho in the background, whose response to the omen is far more important.

multo post – *post* is adverbial here, while *multo* is ablative of measure of difference ('much after').

significatio . . . convenerat – 'had been agreed as the sign that . . .'.

27.2

digressus – noun (not participle).

sibi – 'by him', a dative of agent. This is a usage of the dative more often found in poetry; in prose the agent is usually expressed by a/ab + ablative (although the agent of a gerundive is usually dative even in prose).

eoque – 'and therefore'.

finxisset – 'fabricated (the excuse) that . . .'.

AS

Tiberianam domum – palace built by Tiberius on the Palatine Hill (see n. 17.2 *Palatium*).

Velabrum – a busy commercial area just south of the Forum.

miliarium aureum – a milestone erected by Augustus in 20 BC. It appears to have marked the centre of the empire and the starting point for the major roads of Italy, and may have been inscribed with the distances to important cities.

aedem Saturni – temple at the foot of the Capitoline Hill. Otho's roundabout route seems to have been chosen to disguise his true destination, the praetorian camp.

speculatores – the *speculatores* worked as bodyguards of the emperor alongside the praetorian guard.

alii conscientia ... sumpturi – the word *adgregantur* presents the soldiers as a homogeneous flock (*grex*), but the subsequent appendix reveals the complexity and range of feeling.

animum ... sumpturi – *sumpturi* agrees with *pars* in sense: 'intending to make up their minds based on the outcome'. The interplay of singulars and plurals throughout the appendix again suggests both cohesion and variety.

Chapter 28

stationem ... agebat – 'was on guard', but here meaning 'was the officer in charge of the guard'.

castris – the praetorian camp.

tribunus – see n. 18.3 *tribuni*.

A Level

magnitudine ... metuens – *variatio* with a causal ablative followed by a participle providing an alternative reason.

castra ... exitium – both objects of *metuens.*

corrupta ... castra – 'that the camp had been corrupted' (literally 'the camp having been corrupted ...').

si contra tenderet – literally 'if he exerted himself in opposition', so 'if he resisted'. The subjunctive is suboblique as it represents Martialis' thoughts, and stands for a future indicative in direct speech.

praebuit ... conscientiae – Tacitus does not name his exact actions, but implies that Martialis admitted Otho and the mutineers into the camp.

anteposuere – syncopated form of *anteposuerunt.* This is an archaic ending, which is often seen in poetry and the historians.

praesentia dubiis et honestis – 'the present (situation) to an uncertain and honest (course of action)'.

isque – *is* here is equivalent to *talis*, so *ut* introduces a result clause.

pessimum ... paterentur – this neat *sententia* reveals Tacitus' developed understanding of mob mentality.

Chapter 29

29.1

alieni iam – 'which now belonged to another'.

fatigabat – the implication is that Galba is repeating the ritual until he gets a favourable response.

A Level

cum adfertur – the indicative is used because the *cum*-clause reports the main action, while the grammatical main clause marks the time. This is called an inverted-*cum* clause, and is a construction often used at exciting moments in narratives. *adfertur* is historic present.

rapi . . . raperetur – syntax shifts into indirect speech to report the content of the *rumor* (see n. 17.2 *honorificum*).

incertum quem senatorem – 'some senator or other'. *incertum quis* is sometimes treated as one word and is shorthand for 'some senator, it is uncertain which'. Compare with the more common *nescio quis* which has similar meaning.

simul . . . fuerat – Tacitean *brevitas* adds to the pace of the action here. The subject is in *ut quisque* ('whoever', see n. 26.1 *ut*), a verb must be supplied ('brought reports'), and understand *Othoni* after *obvius fuerat*: 'at the same time whoever encountered Otho brought reports from over the whole city'. The pluperfect is the usual tense for indefinite (*-ever*) clauses in the past.

minora vero – '(making things out to be) less than they truly were'. A participle needs to be supplied in translation, and *vero* is an ablative of comparison (literally 'than the truth').

integra . . . servabatur – 'was kept intact'. Both *integra* and *remediis* have medical associations.

29.2

Piso's speech testing the loyalty of the troops does a lot to develop Tacitus' characterization of him. He misjudges some comments and comes across as disingenuous on a few occasions (see notes below), but his speech is not a complete failure as only the *speculatores* defect (on whom see n. 27.2 *speculatores*).

**A
Level**

It would be worth looking at this speech in conjunction with the two other speeches in Chapters 1–49: Galba's adoption speech (Chapters 15–16) and Otho's speech to the praetorians (Chapters 37–38). Consider the similarities and differences between Tacitus' presentation of each character, and also think about whether the way they describe each other is supported by their behaviour in the narrative.

sextus dies agitur . . . ex quo – 'it is five days since'. Literally 'the sixth day is passing from the one on which', remembering that the Romans counted inclusively (n. 12.1 *paucis*).

commilitones – an attempt to ingratiate himself with the soldiers, but not true since Piso had not held a position in the army. According to Suetonius (*Aug.* 25) Augustus did not use the term, or allow it to be used by his male relatives, as it entailed too much deference to the troops.

et sive – *et* is used to introduce the parenthesis and best omitted in translation.

Caesar – 'as a Caesar'; see n. 5.1 *longo*.

quo . . . positum est – *quo . . . fato* is an indirect question and *adscitus sim* should be supplied. Literally 'it has been placed in your hand with what fate of our household and the state I was adopted', so 'whether I was adopted for the good or the bad . . . has been placed in your hands'.

non quia . . . – with the subjunctive to reject a potential reason behind a statement: '(I say this) not because . . .'.

meo nomine – 'on my own account'.

ut qui . . . discam – *ut qui* + subjunctive = 'because' (causal relative).

cum maxime – 'just at this moment'.

minus discriminis – 'less danger', *discriminis* is partitive genitive (literally 'less of danger').

A Level

solacium ... urbem – 'as a solace in the last disturbance we had a city free from bloodshed'. This is a reference to the massacre at the Milvian Bridge (see n. 6.2 *trucidatis*). Piso is being disingenuous to win the loyalty of the troops, although the bridge was technically outside the city.

res ... translatas – '(the fact that) government was transferred'.

provisum adoptione videbatur ut ... – 'it seemed to have been seen to by the adoption that ...' (with *esse* supplied) or 'adoption seemed to ensure that ...'.

post Galbam – after Galba's death.

Chapter 30

30.1

nihil adrogabo mihi nobilitatis – 'I will not claim to possess any nobility ...'. *nobilitatis* and *modestiae* are partitive genitives (literally 'nothing of nobility') as above in n. 29.2 *minus*. Piso is using a rhetorical device called *praeteritio*, by claiming he will not mention something in order to draw attention to it. For Piso's nobility see 14.2.

vitia – abstract noun as subject, emphasizing the extent to which Otho's vices are in control of his actions.

evertere – take as syncopated form of *everterunt*. Piso is referring to Otho's actions under Nero.

ageret – 'was playing the part of', a theatrical metaphor.

habitune ... ornatu – Tacitus had called Otho *mollis* at 22.1, while Suetonius (*Otho* 12) claims that Otho was bandy-legged and effeminate in his grooming habits.

mereretur – potential subjunctive, expressing a possibility ('could', 'would', 'may', 'might'). The imperfect tense implies the question is now

A Level

closed: 'would he have deserved . . . ?'. Other uses of the subjunctive as a main verb include jussive ('let him go'), optative ('if only he would go') and deliberative ('should I go?').

falluntur quibus – the antecedent of *quibus* is the subject of *falluntur* (general 'they').

iste – pronoun often used contemptuously.

sciet – future tense implies 'if he became emperor'.

penes ipsum sit – 'are in his hands' or 'fall to him'. *sit* is best taken as a suboblique subjunctive as Piso is reporting Otho's thoughts. He is therefore suggesting that Otho is conscious of the disgrace his depravity will bring to the Roman people.

30.2

Galbam . . . dixit – *dixit* (here 'declared') and *Caesarem* ('as Caesar') should be repeated in both parts of this sentence.

generis humani – Piso is exaggerating.

vestra . . . interest ne – 'it is your concern that . . . not'. The impersonal verb *interest* takes the genitive of person concerned, but instead of the personal pronouns uses *mea, tua, sua, nostra* or *vestra*.

Nero . . . vos destituit – this refers to Nero's plans (never carried out) to flee from Rome to Egypt.

30.3

minus triginta – after *minus* and *plus, quam* is often omitted ('less than').

quos . . . nemo ferret – 'whom no one would have tolerated', potential subjunctive (see n. 30.1 *mereretur*).

A Level

admittitis – 'are you going to allow', rhetorical use of the present with future meaning.

commune crimen facitis – literally 'make the crime common', so 'take a share of the crime'.

ad nos scelerum exitus, bellorum ad vos – chiastic arrangement to emphasize the mutual suffering which will result.

ad . . . pertinebunt – 'will affect' (literally 'will relate to').

nec est plus quod . . . quam quod . . . datur – 'what (is offered) . . . is not more than what is offered . . .'.

proinde . . . donativum . . . quam – 'just as big a donative . . . as'. This vague promise was unlikely to have much effect on the soldiers, since Galba had so far neglected to pay them anything (see n. 5.1 *donativum*).

Chapter 31

31.1

non aspernata contionantem – hardly an enthusiastic show of support.

rapit – many of the verbs in this chapter are historic present.

insidiis et simulatione – 'with a treacherous pretence (of loyalty)', intended to deceive Piso and Galba. This is an example of *hendiadys*, a rhetorical device whereby two words, joined by 'and', express one idea. A famous example is Shakespeare's 'a tale . . . full of sound and fury', rather than the less emphatic 'furious sound' (*Macbeth*).

31.2

missus et – supply *est*, and *et* means 'also'.

A Level

Celsus Marius – see n. 14.1 *Mario*. He is sent because he had commanded a legion in *Pannonia*, one of the provinces of *Illyricum*.

Vipsania in porticu – 'in the Vipsanian Colonnade', on the Campus Martius, north-west of the city centre.

praeceptum – impersonal passive, with *est* supplied.

primipilaribus – 'ex-centurions of the first rank'. A *primus pilus* was the chief centurion of a legion. Little is known about the men themselves or the tribunes mentioned later.

Libertatis atrio – 'the Hall of Liberty', at the north of the Capitoline Hill. The site of official archives and a public library.

legioni classicae diffidebatur – intransitive verbs (including verbs which take the dative) must be used impersonally in the passive (*Oxford Latin Grammar*, pp. 106–107). Literally 'it was not trusted to the legion of marines', and therefore 'the legion of marines was not trusted'. For the 'legion of marines' see n. 6.2 *trucidatis*.

si . . . – to see if . . .'.

31.3

adorti – supply *sunt*.

non ordine militiae, sed e Galbae amicis – 'not because of military rank but (because he was one) of Galba's friends'.

et . . . suspectior – 'and (therefore) more suspicious'.

nihil – used adverbially here and stronger than *non*: 'not at all'.

adiungitur – 'joined'. The passive of *adiungo* is used reflexively to mean 'connect oneself' or simply 'join'.

vexilla diu nutavere – 'detachments wavered for a long time', implying they turned against Galba eventually. A *vexillum* is properly a military

A Level

ensign comprising a piece of cloth carried on a crossbar and carried by a detachment of troops, and therefore used also to denote the detachment itself. The vocabulary is striking as *nutavere* (for *nutaverunt*) could refer both to teetering standards and the wavering opinions of the troops.

invalidis ... refovebat – in this appendix Tacitus deems it worth explaining why they had some support for Galba, and emphasizing his care for them, while their decision to join the rebellion ultimately is a given.

Alexandriam – in readiness for the expedition to the Caucasus which was called off (see 6.2).

inde rursus – 'and back again from there'.

invalidis ... aegros – perhaps scurvy, but precise details of the sickness are not given.

Chapter 32

32.1

Palatium – here 'the Palatine Hill' (see n. 17.2 *Palatium*).

servitiis – elevated form of *servis* (and in 32.2). After the neutral main clause, the appendix is very critical of the mob.

caedem Othonis et coniuratorum exitium – chiasmus (ABBA structure) which emphasizes the forcefulness of the crowd's demands.

poscentium – n. 4.2 *primo*.

ut si – 'just as if'.

illis iudicium aut veritas – dative + *sum* (*erat* supplied). *veritas* here means 'integrity'.

A Level

quippe . . . postulaturis – *quippe* + participle = 'since'. Tacitus critically foreshadows the crowd's fickle siding with Otho after Galba's death.

licentia adclamationum – 'with a lack of restraint of acclamations', so 'with unrestrained acclamations'.

32.2

duae sententiae – the narrative moves inside the palace.

manendum . . . opponenda . . . firmandos . . . eundum . . . censebat – *censeo* is here followed by gerunds and gerundives (of attraction).

daret – syntax shifts into indirect speech until the end of the chapter. The subjunctive denotes an indirect command and *spatium* is the object of *daret* both times: '(he said) that he should allow time'.

scelera . . . valescere – accusative + infinitive.

impetu – 'with impulsive action'.

eundi . . . facultatem – take *eundi* after *facultatem* and supply *fore*: 'that there would be . . .'.

ultro – 'of his own accord' (i.e. without waiting to be attacked by Otho).

sit . . . paeniteat – *repraesentatio* increases the urgency (see n. 7.2 *postquam*).

regressum – again supply *fore*: 'but that his (possibility of) retreat would be . . .'.

si paeniteat – 'if he regretted it', i.e. if he left straight away and got into trouble.

**A
Level**

Chapter 33

33.1

festinandum – impersonal gerundive of an intransitive verb, with *esse* supplied (see n. 21.2 *agendum* and n. 31.2 *legioni*): 'that they should act quickly'.

ceteris – the vague *ceteris* serves to isolate Vinius, although Laco and Icelus are mentioned later.

antequam cresceret – subjunctive as the meaning is not purely temporal (see n. 7.1 *antequam*).

trepidaturum ... honestum – extended indirect speech. Supply *esse* with *trepidaturum*.

ignaros – either 'people who did not know him' (see 26.1), or 'who were unaware of the plan'.

cunctatione ... segnitia – causal ablatives.

terentium tempus – i.e. people like Vinius.

discat – suboblique, and another example of *repraesentatio*, as are *elanguescat* and *sit* (see n. 7.2 *postquam*).

non expectandum – supply *esse*, another impersonal gerundive (*occurrendum* later is the same). Translate the *ut* clause as 'for Otho to ...'.

compositis castris – although they were not aware, Otho had already pacified the camp.

Capitolium – i.e. to make a sacrifice on becoming emperor.

dum ... cludit – the present indicative is often retained after *dum* in indirect statement. This is said in response to *firmandos aditus* (32.2).

A Level

egregius imperator cum fortibus amicis – sarcastic adjectives to stress how shameful it would be to stay in the palace. The speech reported here is heavily critical of Vinius.

ianua ac limine tenus – *tenus* is always postposed: 'to the extent of a door and threshold'. The point is that the palace was not equipped to deal with a siege.

nimirum – often used sarcastically.

33.2

praeclarum ... auxilium – supply *fore*. This is in response to *opponenda servitia* (32.2) and the emphatic prefix *prae-* increases the sarcasm.

quae plurimum valet – indicative because it is the thought of Tacitus. *indignatio* is the antecedent of *quae*.

elanguescat – with both *consensus* and *indignatio*. *consensus* is repeated sarcastically from Vinius' speech.

intuta quae indecora – 'that (the course) which was dishonourable was (also) dangerous'. Supply *esse* with *intuta*, and *essent* with *indecora*.

occurrendum – supply *esse*.

id ... honestum – supply *fore*.

repugnantem ... exitium – strong vocabulary emphasizes the infighting at this critical juncture.

privati odii pertinacia – *pertinacia* is causal ablative and the personal hatred is for Vinius.

in publicum exitium – '(which led) to the ruin of the state'.

A
Level

Chapter 34

34.1

nec – take the negative with the participle.

speciosiora suadentibus – referring to Laco and Icelus. *speciosus* literally means 'attractive', but also comes to mean something that is superficially attractive, but of little real value (English 'specious'). As often, outward appearances are deceptive.

tamen – after Galba's decision to act, it is surprising that he sends Piso rather than going himself.

praemissus – supply *est*. The prefix shows that Galba was intending to follow, but the *rumor* in 34.2 forestalls this.

iuvenis – supply *erat*.

recenti favore – 'whose popularity was fresh', an ablative of description (like *magno nomine*). Piso had not been received with vast enthusiasm in Chapters 18–19 and Chapter 31, so Tacitus is here presenting the misguided view of Galba and his advisers.

infensus – as often Tacitus expresses a complex idea in only a few words. Piso's hatred for Vinius is useful because: a) Piso would be more willing to carry out a plan that Vinius disapproved of; b) the soldiers and conspirators also hated Vinius so Piso was more likely to be successful; c) Laco and Icelus would be able to mobilize more hatred against Vinius in order to remove him.

quia irati ita volebant – 'since in their anger they (the opponents of Vinius) wished it so', referring primarily to Laco and Icelus.

et facilius de odio creditur – 'and it is easier to believe in hatred' (literally 'it is more easily believed because of hatred'). Tacitus probably means that it is easier for him (and his readers) to believe that Piso

A Level

really did hate Vinius, especially given Vinius' character and his opposition to Piso's adoption. However, he could also mean that people are generally too quick to believe in hatred, which would imply that Piso's hatred was imagined. The statement is difficult to pin down though, so it is best to maintain the ambiguity in translation.

34.2

occisum – supply *esse*. The accusative and infinitive is dependent on *rumor*.

rumor – supply *erat*. Tacitus delays the word *rumor* in order to provide the news of Otho's death first, before undermining its reliability at the end of the phrase. This suggests the difficulty of knowing what to trust in such turbulent times.

ut in magnis mendaciis – 'as is natural with lies of great importance'.

credula fama – 'since Rumour is gullible'. *fama* is personified here and presented as believing false reports and spreading them around the crowd.

compositum auctumque – supply *esse*.

mixtis iam Othonianis – 'by the partisans of Otho who had now been mixed (into the crowd)', a dative of agent (see n. 27.2 *sibi*).

falso – adverb.

vulgaverint – suboblique subjunctive, perfect tense because of *repraesentatio*.

Chapter 35

35.1

non . . . tantum . . . sed – 'not only . . . but (also)'.

populus . . . imperita plebs – *populus* properly refers to the people as a whole, but it is sometimes used to refer to everyone except the *plebs* (see also 40.1). Tacitus often uses the two words to distinguish between the more and less reputable parts of the population. The *plebs* are described here as 'inexperienced' because under the Principate they were not used to playing an active political role in the state.

ruere . . . ostentare . . . scire . . . adfirmare – historic infinitives (see n. 23.1 *agnoscere*) increase the pace.

ruere – an example of *syllepsis*, where the same verb is used in both metaphorical ('burst into applause . . .') and literal senses ('rushed inside').

ostentare – frequentative of *ostendo*, implying repeated action. This stresses the insistence and number of those trying to gratify Galba.

praereptam – supply *esse*. *sibi* is a dative of disadvantage (see n. 20.2 *quibus*).

ignavissimus quisque – see n. 20.1 *rapacissimo*. Although grammatically singular, the phrase agrees in sense with the plurals *nimii* and *feroces*.

nimii verbis, linguae feroces – this idea is emphasized by the chiastic word order, but there is also *variatio* with the ablative *verbis* and the genitive of reference *linguae* ('fierce of tongue').

donec . . . levaretur – the subjunctive is used in a temporal clause with no further effect on the meaning (see n. 7.1 *antequam*).

**A
Level**

inopia veri et consensu errantium – an interesting phrase that blurs Galba's perspective (*consensu*) with that of Tacitus (*inopia veri* and *errantium*).

victus – a particularly strong choice of word, emphasizing Galba's capitulation.

inruenti turbae – dative governed by *resistens*.

sella – ablative of instrument ('by a chair') but better in English as 'lifted up on a chair'.

35.2

obvius – '(meeting him) on his way'. Latin usually uses connectives (*et, tum, deinde*, connecting relative, etc.) to join sentences. The absence of one (asyndeton) here increases the pace.

Iulius Atticus – only mentioned here.

occisum – supply *esse*. Atticus is, of course, lying.

insigni animo ... incorruptus – Tacitus draws a conclusion from Galba's words here. In English this is made clearer by adding 'showing how he was a man of ...'. *insigni animo* is an ablative of description.

insigni animo ad coercendam – 'of remarkable spirit in restraining ...'.

minantibus ... incorruptus – there is *variatio* in the cases of the participles. Also, note again Tacitus' love of adjectives with the negating prefix *in-*. Here it suggests that Galba's incorruptibility was unusual for the time.

Chapters 36–44 narrate the climax of the rebellion. Otho makes a speech, further inflaming the soldiers in the camp, who he then arms and orders to march on the Forum fearing that Galba has armed the citizens. The deaths of Galba, Titus Vinius and Piso are all described in detail, and their heads are fixed on poles.

**A
Level**

Chapter 36

36.1

haud dubiae . . . mentes – supply *erant*.

tantusque ardor – supply *erat*.

non contenti agmine et corporibus – literally 'not satisfied with the column of men and their bodies', but best taken as 'not satisfied with carrying him on their shoulders in a procession'.

in suggestu – '(placing him) on a platform . . .'. This was a platform in the centre of the camp, from which a leader could address his troops. It held a statue of the emperor and was surrounded by military standards (see below).

Galbae statua – the statue of Galba is now replaced with the real Otho.

inter signa . . . vexillis – a *signum* ('standard') was a pole covered in metal discs and other decorations to represent honours won in battle. The soldiers now also plant their *vexilla* (see n. 31.3 *vexilla*) around the platform.

locus – supply *erat*.

gregarius miles . . . iubebat – a shocking inversion of usual military order.

caveri . . . praepositos – literally 'that the officers be taken heed of . . .', or make active 'people to watch out for the officers'. For the officers' loyalty to Galba, see n. 18.3 *tribuni*.

36.2

strepere . . . – another string of historic infinitives (watch out for the deponent *complecti*).

A Level

exhortatione mutua – another sign of the breakdown in military order. Soldiers are driving each other on, rather than being exhorted by their commanders.

non . . . plebe – 'not like in (a gathering of) the people and plebs': see n. 35.1 *populus*.

variis segni adulatione vocibus – 'when there are shouts which vary in their lazy flattery'. The point is that the soldiers' cries are not varied, and their praise of Otho is not half-hearted.

ut quemque . . . aspexerant – *ut quemque* means 'whoever', and for the pluperfect see n. 29.1 *simul*.

armis – from *armus, -i*, rather than *arma, -orum*. Otho orders weapons to be distributed in Chapter 38.

36.3

nec deerat . . . adorare – 'did not fail to venerate'.

adorare vulgum – *adoro* is elsewhere used of worshipping the gods, or paying homage to kings or emperors, but is followed by the harshly critical word *vulgus* ('mob', 'rabble'). This juxtaposition draws attention to Otho's degrading and insincere efforts to win support. *vulgus* is usually neuter, but is sometimes taken as a masculine second declension, as here.

omnia – supply *facere*.

pro dominatione – 'for the sake of' or 'to obtain supremacy'. The contrast with *serviliter* is heavily critical of Otho.

classicorum legio – for the legion of marines see n. 6.2 *trucidatis*.

viribus – the plural of *vis* usually refers to physical strength.

sacramentum eius accepit – 'took the oath of loyalty to him'. For the genitive see n. 5.1 *Caesarum*.

A Level

quos . . . extimulaverat – supply *eos*.

accendendos – supply *esse*.

ratus – the perfect participle of *reor* is used with present sense.

in commune – 'as a group'.

Chapters 37–38: Otho's speech to the soldiers begins by stressing how their fates are now tied. He recalls Galba's slaughter of the marines and the unpaid donative, criticizes Vinius and Piso, and claims that the senate and the Roman people are depending on them. The speech also describes how Galba has subverted language, calling his punishments 'discipline', his cruelty 'strictness' and his greed 'frugality'. Here Tacitus shows a keen understanding of the importance of language as an instrument of political control, and of the way in which it is contested by people with different claims to power.

At the end of Chapter 38 Otho orders the armoury to be opened. Tacitus provides a fabulous description of the soldiers wildly rushing to arms which captures perfectly the disintegration of military order.

Chapter 39

39.1

Piso . . . adsecutus erat – Piso had been sent ahead to the camp in Chapter 34. The details of his decision to turn back are left vague, with Tacitus instead focusing on his fear. He also skirts over the route that he takes to 'catch up with' Galba. The lack of detail adds to the pace and confusion of the scene.

in urbem usque resonantibus – for the location of the praetorian camp see n. 17.2 *castris*.

A Level

egressum interim – i.e. having left the palace. Again Tacitus packs a lot of information into a few words, giving a sense of the fast-moving action.

Marius Celsus – sent to the Illyrian troops in Chapter 31.

cum alii . . . censerent – 'while some were recommending'.

rostra occupanda – supply *esse*, and for *rostra* see n. 17.2 *pro*.

in consiliis infelicibus – 'when plans are turning out badly'.

optima ... effugerat – literally '(things) whose time had passed seemed best', i.e. 'the best options seemed to be those for which the opportunity had already passed'.

39.2

agitasse – syncopated form.

seu – 'or because'. There is *variatio* with *seu, sive* and *vel*, and with the constructions that follow each.

conscium – '(that he was) an accomplice'.

ad postremum – 'finally', emphasizing *odio*.

odio – causal ablative.

initio ... modus – supply *est*. Literally 'with a beginning of killing having arisen, an end is difficult', and therefore 'when killing has begun, it is difficult to stop', a neat *sententia*.

turbavere – syncopated form.

A Level

Chapter 40

40.1

fluctuantis – storm imagery gives a sense of the movement of the crowd back and forth, but also of the turbulent atmosphere.

basilicis – 'public halls'. There were large multi-purpose buildings that were usually rectangular and open on one side.

neque ... non quies – note the urgency created by piling up short phrases, each with parts of the verb 'to be' omitted.

populi aut plebis – see n. 35.1 *populus*.

quale ... est – '(but there was) the type of silence which is (characteristic) of great fear and great anger'. The expectant tension in the air is palpable.

nuntiabatur – impersonal passive, which emphasizes the lack of credible source. It is actually untrue that the plebs are being armed.

occupare pericula – clever use of vocabulary here, as *occupare* can mean both 'seize upon' and 'forestall'. Is it the soldiers' motive to bring danger or to prevent it? Tacitus is again using ambiguity to engage us more in the reading process.

iubet – supply 'his followers' as the object, and note the historic present (also *inrumpunt* later).

40.2

Vologaesum ... Pacorum ... Arsacidarum – Vologaesus was the king of Parthia during AD 51–78, and was succeeded by his brother Pacorus. They were both part of the Arsacid dynasty ('the *Arsacidae*') founded by Arsaces in 250 BC. The Parthian kingdom was centred in what is now northern Iraq, and they had been considered Rome's

**A
Level**

worst enemy since their crushing defeat of the Romans at Carrhae in 53 BC. The fact that the soldiers are riding against an old, vulnerable Roman emperor as if he were such a formidable foe, shows Tacitus' scorn at the events. Equally, the reference to the 'ancestral throne' of the *Arsacidae* reminds the reader how short-lived Galba's line is to be.

quasi . . . depulsuri . . . pergerent – note the *variatio* of the two words following *quasi* (for the subjunctive see n. 17.1 *quasi*).

trucidare – for the vocabulary see n. 6.2 *trucidatis*.

inrumpunt – historic present.

priores et futuri principes – '(the thought of) past emperors and of those to come'. These thoughts may have been elicited by the statues of past emperors in the Forum. Tacitus' outrage at the events is emphasized by *polysyndeton* as he lists all the symbols of Roman power and religion that the soldiers ignore.

terruere quo minus facerent – *terruere* is syncopated, and for *quo minus* see n. 18.1 *terruit*.

scelus cuius ultor est quisquis successit – literally 'a crime whose avenger is whoever succeeds', and so 'which must be avenged by whoever is the successor'. The present *est* presents this as natural and inevitable, while the perfect is used in indefinite (*-ever*) clauses when the main verb is present. For clarification of the idea expressed here see n. 44.2 *munimentum*.

Chapter 41

41.1

Atilium Vergilionem – only known in relation to this defection.

Galbae imaginem – medallions representing the emperor were attached to the *vexilla* and *signa*.

A Level

manifesta – supply *erant*

in Othonem . . . studia – 'enthusiasm for Otho'.

desertum . . . destricta – supply parts of 'to be'.

41.2

iuxta Curtii lacum – the *Lacus Curtius* was a dried out pit in the Forum. There are a number of myths explaining the origin of its name, but the most important is the story of Marcus Curtius. He was said to have ridden into a chasm that had opened in the Forum, obeying an oracle in order to save Rome. While his death contributed to the survival of the state, Galba's death in the same place ushers in more chaos and turmoil.

ut cuique . . . fuit – 'depending on the hatred or admiration which each person had for him' (dative + *sum*).

varie prodidere – syncopated form of *prodiderunt*; the subject is 'people' in general.

alii suppliciter interrogasse – supply *prodiderunt eum* (also after *plures* below). *interrogasse* is a syncopated form of *interrogavisse*.

quid mali – *mali* is partitive genitive (see n. 29.2 *minus*). Literally 'what of bad', so 'what harm'.

exolvendo donativo – *exolvendo* = *exsolvendo,* a dative gerundive of purpose (see n. 6.2 *opprimendis*).

agerent ac ferirent – '(saying that) they should come and strike him'. The subjunctives are used for an indirect command in the extended indirect speech.

si ita e re publica videretur – 'if that seemed to be for the good of the state'. *videretur* is suboblique, and *esse* should be supplied.

A Level

41.3

non satis constat – 'there is not much agreement'.

quidam – 'some (said that it was) . . .'.

Terentium evocatum – *evocatum* is ambiguous. It usually means a 'veteran' who has rejoined the army under special terms of service, but Galba also often uses the term for his elite bodyguard. The latter would add to the sense of betrayal.

Camurium quintae decimae legionis – the fifteenth legion was stationed in Vetera in Lower Germany.

hausisse – means 'to draw (water)' and therefore 'to pierce' with a weapon to draw blood.

laniavere – syncopated form of *laniaverunt*.

adiecta – supply *sunt*.

Chapter 42

invasere – for *invaserunt*.

de quo et ipso – 'about whom also', i.e. as well as the doubt about Galba's last words.

consumpseritne – equivalent to *utrum consumpserit*. Note the powerful use of the abstract noun *metus* as the subject of this very tangible verb.

esse . . . mandatum – impersonal passive.

quod – connecting relative.

huc . . . inclinat, ut . . . – *ut* introduces a result clause following on from *huc* (literally 'to the point . . . that'). Translate as 'but his life and reputation incline me rather to believe that . . .'.

A Level

cuius causa erat – 'which he was a cause of', because he was one of the main reasons for the praetorians' discontent.

aedem divi Iulii – a temple built by Augustus in the south-east of the Forum, where Julius Caesar had been cremated.

in utrumque latus – literally 'in both sides', but translate as 'through one side and out the other'.

transverberatus – supply *est*.

Chapter 43

43.1

insignem – an emphatic and arresting word placement, especially coming after the description of the wicked Vinius' death. Finally one of the virtuous acts promised in the preface!

illa die – *dies* is often feminine when it refers to a specific day.

aetas nostra vidit – striking personification to emphasize the exemplarity of Densus' actions.

vertendo – *variatio* with the preceding participles and the gerund here. See n. 23.1 *memoria* on the closeness of these two parts of speech.

quamquam vulnerato – Cicero and earlier writers always use *quamquam* to introduce a clause with a finite verb, and not with a single participle as here (see also n. 5.2 *quamvis*).

effugium – 'the chance of escape'.

43.2

Piso . . . trucidatur – a particularly long sentence. It may be prudent to break it into smaller sentences in translation. One approach would

A Level

be to start new sentences at *non religione* and *a quibus* (although a bit of manipulation is required to provide fluent English).

aedem Vestae – Piso manages to reach the south-west of the Forum. The Temple of Vesta contained the sacred fire which was tended by the Vestal Virgins. It also housed the Palladium, a wooden statue of Athena that was said to have protected Troy before it was brought to Rome by Aeneas.

publici servi – probably the temple attendant (*aedituus*). Slaves who carried out religious duties were the property of the state.

contubernio eius – 'in his dwelling'.

non religione nec caerimoniis – 'not because of the sanctity (of the place) and its rites'. The belief in religious buildings as places that can offer sanctuary and protection to those in need has persisted into modern times. Piso's assassins, however, are not delayed by any religious scruples, but because he is well hidden.

inminens – neuter agreeing with *exitium*.

cum advenere – an inverted *cum*-clause, see n. 29.1 *cum* (*advenere* = *advenerunt*).

missu Othonis – literally 'by the sending of Otho', but translate as 'sent by Otho'. *missu* is ablative (fourth declension).

ardentis – take with *Othonis*.

Sulpicius Florus . . . Statius Murcus – both known only for this act. The betrayal of Galba is emphasized by mentioning Sulpicius' recent enfranchisement as a Roman citizen as well as Statius' role as a *speculator* (see n. 27.2 *speculatores*).

civitate – foreigners who were enrolled as legionary soldiers automatically became Roman citizens, which provided them with a

**A
Level**

range of rights and legal protections, but those in auxiliary units usually had to wait until the end of their service (twenty-five years).

in foribus templi – Sulpicius and Murcus' lack of religious scruples, alluded to earlier, are shockingly portrayed here. Not only is Piso dragged out of the temple, but he is slaughtered in front of it like a sacrificial animal.

trucidatur – historic present. For the vocabulary see n. 6.2 *trucidatis*.

Chapter 44

44.1

nullam . . . dicitur – i.e. than Piso's. Note the repetition of *nullam . . . nullum* to stress Otho's joy.

perlustrasse – syncopated form. The prefix *per-* suggests the intensity with which Otho stared at the head.

seu . . . seu – 'either because . . . or because'.

in Galba . . . in Tito Vinio – *in* here means 'in the case of . . .'.

recordatio maiestatis – recollection of Galba's imperial majesty reminds Otho that he has committed treason.

amicitiae – repeat *recordatio* here.

Pisonis . . . credebat – supply 'but'. This *asyndeton*, especially after the repetition and balanced phrases earlier in the sentence, has a disarming effect, which draws attention to Otho's unreasonable justification of his satisfaction at Piso's death.

ut – 'as he was'.

ius fasque – 'that it was lawful and right', with *esse* supplied. *ius* refers to what is sanctioned by law, and *fas* that which is ordained

A Level

by the gods. Both words are nouns but often best translated as adjectives.

44.2

praefixa ... legionis – this is a shocking image. Bloody heads on poles are paraded by the soldiers among the legionary standards, important symbols of Roman military discipline and order.

cohortium ... legionis – referring, respectively, to the Praetorian Guard and the legion of marines. The merging of very different units adds to the sense of corrupted military order.

aquilam – each legion had one standard topped by an eagle made of silver or gold, and covered in wreaths. It symbolized the spirit of the legion and was treated with religious respect, which makes its inclusion here even more appalling.

certatim ostentantibus cruentas manus qui ... – each following *qui* refers back to *ostentantibus*. In translation it is easiest to take the relatives first and leave this phrase till last: 'while those who ... vied with each other in exhibiting their bloody hands'. The appendix further highlights the sense of distorted military order: the fact that all the soldiers are vying to prove their loyalty and commitment is undercut by the nature of the crime they are claiming, and that many are claiming it falsely.

qui ... – repetition of *qui* at the beginning of each clause (*anaphora*) and *asyndeton* emphasize the numbers claiming responsibility for the murders.

ut – 'on the grounds that it was'.

non honori – 'not for the sake of honouring', dative of purpose.

munimentum ... ultionem – the accusatives are in apposition to Vitellius' orders: 'as a protection for the time being, and a (means of

A Level

getting) vengeance in the future'. The point is (as at 40.2) that an emperor should punish the murderers of a predecessor, both to remove potential conspirators ('protection'), and to encourage future emperors to do the same if they themselves are assassinated ('vengeance'). Vitellius, who is executed by Vespasian's soldiers in December AD 69, in fact fails on both counts.

Chapters 45–48: Tacitus describes the immediate aftermath of the rebellion. There are numerous displays of flattery from the senate and the people, and the will of the soldiers reigns supreme. Laco is exiled, then assassinated, and Icelus is publicly executed. Piso and Titus Vinius are both buried by their families, and Tacitus gives both an obituary in Chapter 48.

Chapter 49

Chapter 49 mainly comprises Galba's obituary. Tacitus gives a wide-ranging survey of his career, and also picks out some of the key features of his personality and ability as a ruler. As you read it, consider whether Tacitus' obituary of Galba presents him in a positive or negative light, and whether it matches with his presentation of Galba earlier in the narrative.

49.1

licentia tenebrarum – 'because of the licence which darkness provides'.

e prioribus servis – '(one) of his former slaves', i.e. a freedman.

per lixas – 'by the camp-followers'. *lixae* were tradesmen who followed an army and sold goods to the soldiers, and *per* here is equivalent to *a/ab*.

A Level

Patrobii – mentioned also at *Histories* II.95 as a particularly corrupt individual.

49.2

quinque principes . . . emensus – Galba was born in AD 4, during the reign of Augustus. He had therefore lived under all of the Julio-Claudian emperors (Augustus, Tiberius, Caligula, Claudius and Nero).

felicior – supply the imperfect of *esse* here and with the following clauses up to *dum vigebat*.

vetus . . . nobilitas – Galba even claimed that his lineage stretched back to Jupiter on his father's side and Minos on his mother's. For more detail see Suetonius *Galba* 2–3.

magnae opes – according to Plutarch (*Galba* 3.1) Galba was the richest private person who came to the imperial throne.

ipsi medium ingenium – 'his own character was middling'. This is explained further by the pithy epigram *magis . . . virtutibus*.

49.3

amicorum libertorumque – with both *patiens* and *ignarus*. Consider which friends Tacitus could be referring to.

ubi in bonos incidisset – subjunctive of repeated occurrence ('whenever he . . .), a usage not found in the Classical Latin of Cicero and Caesar.

si mali forent – 'if they were ever bad'. *forent* is subjunctive for the same reason as *incidisset*.

usque ad culpam ignarus – 'blind to a fault'.

metus temporum – take *metus* as nominative plural (fourth declension).

A Level

obtentui – 'served to veil (the truth)'. *obtentui* is predicative dative (see n. 7.3 *inrisui*), and *erat* should be supplied again. The point here is that it was dangerous to be too conspicuous, especially for those of high birth, under emperors like Caligula and Nero. Galba therefore kept a low profile, something that was described by some as 'wisdom', but according to Tacitus was really 'inactivity'.

quod – the antecedent is an unexpressed *id*: 'that which was ...'.

49.4

dum vigebat aetas – literally 'while his age was vigorous', so 'in his prime of life'.

apud Germanias – 'in the German provinces'. Galba served as the *legatus* (governor) of Upper Germany (AD 40–42). *apud* simply meaning 'in' is rare in earlier writers (and more common in the *Annals*).

pro consule – 'as *proconsul*'. A *legatus* (technically a *legatus Augusti propraetore*) governed the imperial provinces (see above), while a *proconsul* was the governor in the senatorial provinces (where, in theory, the senate rather than the emperor chose the governor). Galba held his post in Africa in AD 44–45. *Proconsuls* were originally magistrates who governed provinces 'in the place of the consul', due to the difficulty of their being managed from Rome, usually straight after they had held the consulship.

citeriorem Hispaniam – refers properly to *Hispania Terraconensis* (the province of *Hispania Citerior* had ceased to exist in AD 27), an area covering all of modern-day Spain except Andalucia. Galba governed here from AD 60 until he was approached by Vindex in AD 68.

omnium consensu capax imperii nisi imperasset – an astute and cleverly constructed *sententia*. The omission of *esse* from the first part

A Level

of the conditional suggests that everyone *did* believe he was capable of ruling (not 'would have believed') but that this perception was shattered when he actually came to power. Translate as: 'in the agreement of all capable of ruling – had he not been emperor'. *imperasset* is a syncopated form.

Glossary of Names

Information is given about individuals in the commentary notes, but for quick reference a glossary of names has been provided. For places referred to in the text, refer to the commentary notes as well as the maps that come after the Introduction.

NB: Names are listed as Tacitus gives them in the text, ordered alphabetically by *nomen* and *cognomen*. Where Tacitus provides a praenomen it is given in abbreviated form with no effect on the alphabetical order.

Aemilius Pacensis	*Military tribune dismissed by Galba*
Albani	*Caspian tribe against which Nero organized a military expedition*
Amullius Serenus	*Primus pilus under Galba*
Antonius Naso	*Military tribune dismissed by Galba*
Antonius Taurus	*Military tribune dismissed by Galba*
Apollo	*God of Prophecy, the Arts and the Sun*
Argius	*Galba's steward*
Arsacidae	*Parthian dynasty*
Atilius Vergilio	*Standard bearer said to have been first of those escorting Galba to desert*
(Divus) Augustus	*First emperor of Rome, deified after his death*
Caesar	*Title given to all emperors in honour of Julius Caesar*
Camurius	*Soldier most commonly said to have killed Galba*
Cetrius Severus	*Military tribune under Galba*
Cingonius Varro	*Consul-elect for AD 69 put to death by Galba*
Clodius Macer	*Legionary commander of Africa ordered to death by Galba*
Cornelius Aquinus	*Legionary commander who put Fonteius Capito to death*
Cornelius Laco	*Praetorian prefect appointed by Galba, known for his ineffectiveness*

M. Crassus	*Father of Piso*
M. Curtius	*Legendary figure who is said to have ridden into the Lacus Curtius*
Domitius Sabinus	*Primus pilus under Galba*
Ducenius Geminus	*City prefect present at Piso's adoption*
Fabius Valens	*Legionary commander who put Fonteius Capito to death*
Fonteius Capito	*Governor of Lower Germany put to death under unclear circumstances*
Ser. Galba	*Emperor from June AD 68 to January AD 69*
Icelus	*Galba's freedman*
(Divus) Julius	*Julius Caesar, who was deified after his death*
Julius Atticus	*Member of Galba's bodyguard who falsely claimed to have killed Galba*
Julius Carus	*Legionary soldier who killed Titus Vinius*
Julius Fronto	*Military tribune dismissed by Galba*
Julius Martialis	*Officer in charge in the praetorian camp on the day of Galba's death*
Laecanius	*Soldier, one of those rumoured to be Galba's killer*
Marcianus	*Equestrian name given to Icelus, Galba's freedman*
Marius Celsus	*Consul-elect and friend of Galba*
Nero	*Emperor of Rome AD 54–68*
Nymphidius Sabinus	*Praetorian prefect who first sided with Galba. He then declared himself emperor and was put to death by his own troops*
Octavia	*Nero's wife*
Onomastus	*Otho's freedman, an important player in his conspiracy*
M. Otho	*Leader of the conspiracy against Galba, and emperor of Rome January–April AD 69*
Pacorus	*King of Parthia AD 78–105*
Patrobius	*Freedman of Nero, put to death by Galba*
Petronius Turpilianus	*Consul in AD 61 put to death by Galba*
Piso Licinianus	*Young nobleman chosen by Galba as his successor*
Pompeius Longinus	*Military tribune under Galba*

Pompeius Propinquus	*Procurator in Belgic Gaul*
Poppaea Sabina	*Nero's courtesan, who had also been involved with Otho*
Ptolemaeus	*One of Otho's astrologers*
Rubellius Plautus	*Great-grandson of Tiberius, executed by Nero in AD 62*
Saturn	*Father of Jupiter, king of the Gods*
Scribonia	*Mother of Piso*
Sempronius Densus	*Centurion who showed bravery by protecting Piso from Otho's troops*
Statius Murcus	*Piso's killer*
Subrius Dexter	*Military tribune under Galba*
Sulpicius Florus	*Piso's killer*
Terentius	*Veteran and one of three rumoured to be Galba's killer*
Tiberius	*Second Roman emperor, in power during AD 14–37*
Trebonius Garutianus	*Procurator who put Clodius Macer to death under Galba's orders*
Umbricius	*Soothsayer*
Vesta	*Goddess of the Hearth whose temple housed the flame of Rome*
Vindex	*Governor of Gaul who revolted from Nero in AD 68 and encouraged Galba to declare himself emperor*
T. Vinius	*Galba's co-consul, known for his depravity*
A. Vitellius	*Emperor of Rome April–December AD 69*
Vologaesus	*King of Parthia AD 51–78*

Glossary of Technical Terms

The following glossary is designed to provide help with a range of technical terms that appear in the Introduction and Commentary. Terms relating to rhetorical devices are marked in bold for ease of reference, but they should by no means be seen as a complete 'checklist' of terms that students are required to know. Some terms (e.g. proconsul) had different meanings at different times of Roman history, so definitions given here are limited to their usage by Tacitus in *Histories* I. All terms are explained in more detail in the Introduction and Commentary.

Appendix	*An additional phrase after the main verb, a stylistic departure from the period structure of Classical Latin*
Asyndeton	*Omission of a conjunction ('and', 'but') where it would normally be expected*
Brevitas	*Characteristically Tacitean economy of style*
Capitol	*Rome's central temple, to Jupiter Optimus Maximus, on the Capitoline Hill*
Centurion	*Leader of a century*
Century	*Unit of around 100 men*
Client	*A free man in the service of a patron*
Cohort	*Unit of military organization of 500 or 1000 men*
Comitia	*Assembly of the Roman people for electing magistrates*
Consul	*Chief civil and military magistrate of Rome during the Republic. Under the Principate an institution that conferred less power, but still considerable honour*
Decemvir	*Member of the college of priests (decemviri sacris faciundis), with charge of religious affairs pertaining to the state*
Donative	*A gift of money paid by an emperor to each soldier upon his accession or at other special occasions*

Emperor	*A ruler of the Roman Empire*
Equites	*Lower of the two aristocratic classes (the other being the senatorial class)*
Evocatus	*Either a veteran soldier who has rejoined the army or a member of Galba's bodyguard*
Forum	*Main public square of Rome*
Hendiadys	*Expression of one idea using two nouns joined by the word 'and'*
Homoioteleuton	*Use of words with similar endings*
Hypallage	*Transferral of an adjective from the word it really describes onto a different word*
Legatus (Augusti propraetore)	*Governor of an imperial province (one for which the governor was chosen by the emperor)*
Legatus legionis	*Senior commander of a legion*
Legion	*Largest unit of the Roman army, comprising around 5000 men. In AD 69 there were around 30 legions in total*
Litotes	*The use of understatement to emphasize meaning*
Marines	*Soldiers serving in the Roman navy*
Palatine	*The imperial residence, built by Augustus on the Palatine Hill, and used for imperial business*
Patres	*Another name for the senators*
Period	*A typical sentence in Classical Latin, with a subject at the start, main verb at the end and subordinate clauses in between*
Plebs	*The common people of Rome*
Polysyndeton	*Repetition of conjunctions (such as 'both', 'and', etc.)*
Praeteritio	*Rhetorical device by which someone claims they will not mention something in order to draw attention to it*
Praetor	*Magistrate just below consul, with powers relating to civil jurisdiction*
Praetorian Guard	*The only legion stationed permanently in Rome, mainly for the protection of the emperor and the suppression of riots*

Praetorian prefect	*The leader of the Praetorian Guard*
Primus pilus	*The chief centurion of a legion*
Princeps	*Another title for the emperor*
Principate	*The period when the emperors ruled Rome*
Proconsul	*Governor of a senatorial province (where, in theory, the governor was chosen by the senator)*
Procuratores	*Officials employed by the emperor for a range of types of provincial administration*
Province	*Main administrative division of the Roman Empire*
Quaestor	*Junior magistracy with responsibility for financial matters*
Repraesentatio	*Vivid use of tenses in historic sequence which strictly belong to primary sequence*
Republic	*Period of Roman history before the Principate, when Rome was governed by the senate*
Rostra	*Platform in the Forum from which orations and announcements were made*
Senate	*Political body with wide ranging powers in the Republic, which continued to exercise legislative power in the Principate*
Senator	*A member of the Roman senate, who was therefore eligible to hold important political and military roles*
Senatorial class	*Higher of the two aristocratic classes (the other being the equestrian class). Membership was granted to senators and their families*
Sententia	*Pithy, neatly arranged statement that can be removed from a sentence to express a more general truth*
Sesterce	*Roman unit of currency*
Signum	*A Roman military standard*
Speculatores	*Imperial bodyguards*
Suffect consul	*A consul who holds office during the year, but not at the beginning of the year, and therefore does not give his name to the year*

Tmesis	*Splitting up of one word by another (a-whole-nother thing)*
Tribunus	*Commander of a military cohort*
Urban cohorts	*Rome's police force*
Variatio	*Purposeful variation of style and avoidance of balanced sentence structure*
Vexillum	*Either a military ensign consisting of a cloth carried on a crossbar, or to refer to the detachment of troops that carried it*
Vigiles	*Rome's night watch and fire service*

Vocabulary

An asterisk * denotes a word in OCR's Defined Vocabulary List for AS.

* **a/ab (+ abl.)**	by, from
abdo, abdere, abdidi, abditum	hide
absens, -entis	absent
abstineo, abstinere, abstinui, abstentum	abstain from (+ abl.)
ac	and
accedo, accedere, accessi, accessum	approach, add to, be in addition, agree with (+ dat.)
accendo, accendere, accendi, accensum	set on fire, stir up
accerso, accersere, accersii (or -ivi), accersitum	summon
* **accipio, accipere, accepi, acceptum**	take, receive, accept, endure
* **acer, acris, acre**	sharp, fierce, vigorous
Achaia, -ae, f.	Achaia, Greece
actio, -onis, f.	action, lawsuit
actum, i, n.	deed
actus, -us, m.	progress, momentum
* **ad (+ acc.)**	to, towards, for, for the purpose of, in accordance with
ad postremum	finally
adclamatio, -onis, f.	acclamation
* **addo, addere, addidi, additum**	add, assign
adedo, adesse, adedi, adesum	eat up, use up
* **adeo**	so, so greatly
adeo, adire, adii (or -ivi), aditum	go to, approach
adfecto, adfectare, adfectavi, adfectatum	strive after
adfero, adferre, attuli, allatum	bring to, lead to, propose
adfirmo, adfirmare, adfirmavi, adfirmatum	declare, affirm
adfligo, adfligere, adflixi, adflictum	cast down

adfluo, adfluere, adfluxi, adfluxum	flow to, come in haste, flock towards
adgrego, adgregare, adgregavi, adgregatum	cause to flock together; (in passive) flock together
adhibeo, adhibere, adhibui, adhibitum	add to, summon
* **adhuc**	until now, yet, still
adicio, adicere, adieci, adiectum	throw at, add
aditus, -us, m.	entrance
adiungo, adiungere, adiunxi, adiunctum	connect, join
adloquor, adloqui, adlocutus sum	address
administro, administrare, administravi, administratum	manage
admiratio, -onis, f.	admiration
admisceo, admiscere, admiscui, admixtum	join to, put with (+ dat.)
admitto, admittere, admisi, admissum	allow
adnecto, adnectere, adnexui, adnectum	connect to
adoptio, -onis, f.	adoption
adopto, adoptare, adoptavi, adoptatum	adopt
adorior, adoriri, adortus sum	attack
adoro, adorare, adoravi, adoratum	venerate, worship
adpetens, -entis	desirous of (+ gen.)
adpropinquo, adpropinquare, adpropinquavi, adpropinquatum	approach (+ dat.)
adquiro, adquirere, adquisivi, adquisitum	acquire
adrogo, adrogare, adrogavi, adrogatum	claim to protect
adscisco, adsciscere, adscivi, adscitum	admit, adopt
adsequor, adsequi, adsecutus sum	catch up with
adsevero, adseverare, adseveravi, adseveratum	assert strongly

adsigno, adsignare, adsignavi, adsignatum	bestow
adsto, adstare, adstiti	stand
adsuefacio, adsuefacere, adsuefeci, adsuefactum	make accustomed to, condition
adsuetus, -a, -um	accustomed to (+ dat.)
* **adsum, adesse, adfui**	be present
adulatio, -onis, f.	flattery
adulescentia, -ae, f.	youth
adulor, adulari, adulatus sum	flatter
adulterium, -i, n.	adultery
adultus, -a, -um	mature, firmly established
* **advenio, advenire, adveni, adventum**	arrive
* **adversus (+ acc.)**	against, towards
* **adversus, -a, -um**	adverse, unfavourable
aedes, -is, f.	temple
aeger, -gra, -grum	sick
aegre	with difficulty
Aemilius, -i, m.	Aemilius
aemulatio, -onis, f.	emulation
aemulus, -i, m.	rival
aequalis, -e	equal
aeque	equally
aestimatio, -onis, f.	assessment
aetas, -atis, f.	age, life
Africa, -ae, f.	Africa
* **ager, agri, m.**	field, land
agito, agitare, agitavi, agitatum	disturb, consider, discuss
agmen, -inis, n.	march, column (of troops), procession
agnosco, agnoscere, agnovi, agnotum	recognize
* **ago, agere, egi, actum**	do, drive, pass (time), act, play the part of
age, agite (imperative)	come!
alacer, alacris, alacre	eager
Albani, -orum, m. pl.	Albani
Alexandria, -ae, f.	Alexandria
alibi	elsewhere

alienus, -a, -um	belonging to another, someone else's, of others
aliquando	sometimes
aliqui, aliqua, aliquod (adjective)	some
* aliquis, aliquid (pronoun)	anyone, anything, someone, something
* alius, alia, aliud (pronoun or adjective)	some, other, different
* *alii . . . alii . . .*	some . . . others . . .
alo, alere, alui, alitum	nourish
Alpes, -ium, m. pl.	Alps
* alter, -era, -erum (gen. *alterius*)	one . . . the other . . .
alter . . . alter . . .	one . . . the other . . .
* altus, -a, -um	deep
ambigo, -ere	be unsure
ambigitur (impersonal)	there is doubt
ambiguus, -a, -um	ambiguous
ambitiosus, -a, -um	self-serving, ambitious
ambitus, -us, m.	manoeuvring, corruption
amicitia, -ae, f.	friendship
* amicus, -i, m.	friend
* amo, amare, amavi, amatum	love
amolior, amoliri, amolitus sum	remove, get rid of
* amor, -oris, m.	love
Amullius, -i, m.	Amullius
* an	or, or perhaps, whether
anceps, ancipitis	twofold, doubtful, dangerous
ango, angere, anxi, anctum	vex, distress
* animus, -i, m.	mind, spirit, feelings
* annus, -i, m.	year
* ante (+ acc.)	in front of
ante (adverb)	before
antepono, anteponere, anteposui, antepositum	prefer
* antequam	before
antiquitus	in ancient times, traditionally
antiquus, -a, -um	ancient, old-fashioned
Antonius, -i, m.	Antonius
anulus, -i, m.	ring

anxius, -a, -um	anxious, worried
Apollo, -inis, m.	Apollo
appello, appellare, appellavi, appellatum	call, call to payment
* **apud (+ acc.)**	among, with, at the house of, under (a leader); see note 4.2
* **aquila, -ae, f.**	eagle, standard
Aquinus, -i, m.	Aquinus
arbitrium, -i, n.	judgement, power
arbitror, arbitrari, arbitratus sum	think
arcanum, -i, n.	secret
architectus, -i, m.	architect
ardeo, ardere, arsi, arsum	burn, desire ardently
ardor, -oris, m.	enthusiasm
Argius, -i, m.	Argius
* **arma, -orum, n. pl.**	arms, weapons
armatus, -i, m.	armed man
armo, armare, armavi, armatum	arm
armus, -i, m.	arm
Arsacidae, -arum, m. pl.	the Arsacidae
* **ars, artis, f.**	art, skill, practice, conduct, deceit, cunning
aspectus, -us, m.	sight
aspernor, aspernari, aspernatus sum	reject, scorn
aspicio, aspicere, aspexi, aspectum	see
* **at**	but
Atilius, -i, m.	Atilius
atque	and
atrium, -i, n.	hall
atrox, -ocis	dreadful, awful
Atticus, -i, m.	Atticus
* **attonitus, -a, -um**	astonished
auctor, -oris, m.	instigator
auctoritas, -atis, f.	authority
* **audeo, audere, ausus sum**	dare, be daring
* **audio, audire, audivi, auditum**	hear, listen to, hear of
* **aufero, auferre, abstuli, ablatum**	remove, take away, steal
* **augeo, augere, auxi, auctum**	increase, strengthen, exaggerate
Augustus, -i, m.	Augustus

aula, -ae, f.	court, palace
aureus, -a, -um	golden
auris, -is, f.	ear
* **aut**	or
aut . . . aut	either . . . or
* **auxilium, -i, n.**	help, assistance; (pl.) auxiliaries
avaritia, -ae, f.	greed
avarus, -a, -um	stingy
avidus, -a, -um	greedy, eager for (+ gen.)
avitus, -a, -um	ancestral
basilica, -ae, f.	public hall
Belgica, -ae, f.	Belgic Gaul
* **bellum, -i, n.**	war
* **bene**	well
bis	twice
blandior, blandiri, blanditus sum	flatter
* **bona, -orum, n. pl.**	property
* **bonus, -a, -um**	good
brachium, -i, n.	arm
* **brevis, -e**	short
brevi (tempore)	soon
brevitas, -atis, f.	brevity
Britannia, -ae, f.	Britain
Britannicus, -a, -um	British
* **cado, cadere, cecidi, casum**	fall
* **caedes, -is, f.**	death, slaughter, murder, massacre
caelebs, -ibis	bachelor
caerimonia, -ae, f.	religious rite
Caesar, -aris, m.	Caesar, emperor
caelestis, -e	from heaven
callidus, -a, -um	clever
calo, -onis, m.	soldier's attendant
Campania, -ae, f.	Campania
Camurius, -i, m.	Camurius
capax, -acis	capable of, competent (+ gen.)
Capito, -onis, m.	Capito
Capitolium, -i, n.	Capitol, Capitoline Hill

* caput, -itis, n.	head
Carus, -i, m.	Carus
Caspius, -a, -um	Caspian
* castra, -orum, n. pl.	camp
casus, -us, m.	misfortune
* causa, -ae, f.	cause, reason
* caveo, cavere, cavi, cautum	take heed of
celebro, celebrare, celebravi, celebratum	frequent, celebrate
Celsus, -i, m.	Celsus
cena, -ae, f.	dinner
censeo, censere, censui, censum	propose, recommend, vote
centum	a hundred
* centurio, -onis, m.	centurion
* certamen, -inis, n.	contest, enthusiasm
certatim	in rivalry
* certus, -a, -um	certain
* ceteri, -ae, -a	others, the rest
ceterum	but
Cetrius, -i, m.	Cetrius
Cingonius, -i, m.	Cingonius
* circa (+ acc.)	around, with regard to
circumdo, circumdare, circumdedi, circumdatum	surround
circumsto, circumstare, circumsteti	surround
circus, -i, m.	circus
citer, citra, citrum	on this side
citerior Hispania	Hither Spain
* civitas, -atis, f.	state, citizens, citizenship
* clamor, -oris, m.	shout
claritas, -atis, f.	fame
* clarus, -a, -um	glorious
classicus, -a, -um	of marines
classicus, -i, m.	marine
classis, -is, f.	fleet
classibus	in ships, by ship
claustrum, -i, n.	gate
cliens, -entis, m.	client
Clodius, -i, m.	Clodius

cludo, cludere, clusi, clusum	shut up
coalesco, coalescere, coalui, coalitum	grow strong
coeo, coire, coii (or -ivi), coitum	gather
* **coepi, coepisse, coeptum (perfect forms only)**	began, undertook, began to speak
coepto, coeptare, coeptavi, coeptatum	begin, undertake
coeptum, -i, n.	undertaking
coerceo, coercere, coercui, coercitum	restrain, conceal
coetus, -us, m.	gathering
cogitatio, -onis, f.	thought, plan, idea
* **cohors, -ortis, f.**	cohort
* **comes, -itis, m.**	companion
comis, -e	amiable, obliging
comissatio, -onis, f.	drunken revelry
comitatus, -us, m.	attendance, service
comiter	with goodwill
comitia, -orum, n. pl.	assembly, election
comitor, comitari, comitatus sum	accompany
commeatus, -us, m.	supplies
commendo, commendare, commendavi, commendatum	recommend
commilito, -onis, m.	comrade, fellow soldier
comminus	close by
communis, -e	shared, common, in common
comparatio, -onis, f.	comparison
* **comparo, comparare, comparavi, comparatum**	compare
complector, complecti, complexus sum	embrace
compleo, complere, complevi, completum	fill
compono, componere, composui, compositum	arrange, organize, fabricate, pacify
comprobo, comprobare, comprobavi, comprobatum	sanction
comptus, -a, -um	adorned
computo, computare, computavi, computatum	compare
conatus, -us, m.	attempt, undertaking
concieo, conciere, concivi, concitum	rouse, stir

concilio, conciliare, conciliavi, conciliatum	win over
concipio, concipere, concepi, conceptum	conceive, adopt
concupisco, concupiscere, concupisci, concupitum	desire strongly
confido, confidere, confisus sum	put one's trust in (+ dat.)
confiteor, confiteri, confessus sum	confess
confundo, confundere, confudi, confusum	mix together; distress
congruo, congruere, congrui	happen at the same time, coincide
conicio, conicere, conieci, coniectum	turn
coniectura, -ae, f.	conjecture, prophecy
coniuratio, -onis, f.	conspiracy, plot
coniuratus, -i, m.	conspirator
conloco, conlocare, conlocavi, conlocatum	place
conquiro, conquirere, conquisivi, conquisitum	search out
consaluto, consalutare, consalutavi, consalutatum	hail as
conscientia, -ae, f.	knowledge of a plot, complicity, guilt, guilty conscience
conscius, -a, -um	aware, privy to
conscius, -i, m.	accomplice
conscribo, conscribere, conscipsi, conscriptum	enrol, enlist
consensus, -us, m.	agreement, consensus, collective action
consentio, consentire, consensi, consensum	agree
* consilium, -i, n.	plan, purpose
consto, constare, constiti	stand together, be agreed upon
constat (impersonal)	it is agreed, there is agreement
* consul, -ulis, m.	consul
consul designatus	consul-elect
consularis, -e	of consular rank, ex-consul
consulto, consultare, consultavi, consultatum	consult, reflect, discuss

* **consumo, consumere, consumpsi, consumptum**	consume, eat up
contego, contegere, contexi, contectum	cover, bury
contemptor, -oris, m.	hater
contemptus, -us, m.	contempt, scorn
contentus, -a, -um	satisfied
contineo, continere, continui, contentum	hold together, govern
contio, -onis, f.	gathering
contionor, contionari, contoniatus sum	address a crowd, make a speech
* **contra (+ acc.)**	against
contra (adverb)	against, in opposition
contra dico	oppose (+ dat.)
contrarius, -a, -um	opposite
contubernalis, -is, m.	messmate
contubernium, -i, n.	slave dwelling, apartment
contus, -i, m.	pole
convenio, convenire, conveni, conventum	come together, be agreed upon
convenit (impersonal)	it is agreed
converto, convertere, converti, conversum	turn, direct
Cornelius, -i, m.	Cornelius
* **corpus, -oris, n.**	body
corruptus, -a, um	corrupt, depraved
Crassus, -i, m.	Crassus
creber, -bra, -brum	constant, frequent, repeated
crebresco, crebescere, crebui	grow
* **credo, credere, credidi, creditum**	believe
credulus, -a, -um	credulous, gullible
cremo, cremare, cremavi, crematum	burn, cremate
cresco, crescere, crevi, cretum	grow
* **crimen, -inis, n.**	accusation, crime
cruentus, -a, -um	bloody
crus, -uris, n.	leg
* **culpa, -ae, f.**	fault
* **cum**	when, since
cum maxime	just at this moment

* **cum** (+ abl.)	with
cunctatio, -onis, f.	delay, hesitation
cunctor, cunctari, cunctatus sum	delay, hesitate
* **cunctus, -a, -um**	all, every
cupiditas, -atis, f.	desire, greed
cupido, -inis, f.	desire
* **cura, -ae, f.**	care, concern, anxiety
Curtius, -i, m.	Curtius
custodia, -ae, f.	guard, protection
damno, damnare, damnavi, damnatum	condemn
* **de** (+ abl.)	about, of
decimus, -a, -um	tenth
decus, -oris, m.	honour, grace
dedecus, -oris, n.	disgrace, immorality
defectio, -onis, f.	mutiny, rebellion
* **dein**	then
demum	finally
* **denique**	finally
Densus, -i, m.	Densus
depello, depellere, depuli, depulsum	drive away
depono, deponere, deposui, depositum	entrust
deprecor, deprecari, deprecatus sum	pray for
deripio, deripere, deripui, dereptum	tear off
descisco, desciscere, descivi, descitum	rebel
desero, deserere, deserui, desertum	desert
desertor, -oris, m.	deserter
designatus, -a, -um	designate, elect (see *consul*)
destino, destinare, destinavi, destinatum	fix, name, mark out, designate
destituo, destituere, destitui, destitutum	abandon, desert
destringo, destringere, destrinxi, districtum	draw (a weapon)
destruo, destruere, destruxi, destructum	demolish, ruin

desum, deesse, defui	be absent, be lacking, fail, fail to do one's duty
deterior, -ius	less good, worse, more wicked
deus, -i, m.	god
Dexter, -tri, m.	Dexter
dico, dicere, dixi, dictum	say, declare
* **dies, diei, m. or f.**	day
differo, differre, distuli, dilatum	delay
* **difficilis, -e**	difficult
diffido, diffidere, diffisus sum	mistrust (+ dat.)
diffugium, -i, n.	defection
dignatio, -onis, f.	dignity
digredior, digredi, digressus sum	depart
digressus, -us, m.	departure
dilabor, dilabi, dilapsus sum	disperse
dirimo, dirimere, diremi, diremptum	break up
disciplina, -ae, f.	discipline
* **disco, discere, didici**	learn, learn how to (+ inf.)
discordia, -ae, f.	discord, conflict
discors, -cordis	disagreeing, in conflict
discrimen, -inis, n.	danger
disicio, disicere, disieci, disiectum	scatter
dispensator, -oris, m.	steward
dissimulatio, -onis, f.	concealment, pretended ignorance
dissimulo, dissimulare, dissimulavi, dissimulatum	conceal
dissonus, -a, -um	discordant
distineo, distinere, distinui, distentum	hold back
distinguo, distinguere, distinxi, distinctum	distinguish
* **diu**	for a long time
diutius	longer (comparative of *diu*)
diversus, -a, -um	different
* **divido, dividere, divisi, divisum**	divide
divus, -i, m.	god, divine (title applied to deified emperor)
* **do, dare, dedi, datum**	give, allow
* **doceo, docere, docui, doctum**	teach, show

* doleo, dolere, dolui, dolitum	grieve
* dolus, -i, m.	treachery, plot
domesticus, -a, -um	in one's household
dominatio, -onis, f.	supremacy
dominor, dominari, dominatus sum	rule, be in power
Domitius, -i, m.	Domitius
* domus, -us, f.	house, household, palace
donatio, -onis, f.	gift
donativum, -i, n.	donative
donec	until, as long as
dono, donare, donavi, donatum	give, grant, present someone (acc.) with something (abl.)
dubito, dubitare, dubitavi, dubitatum	hesitate
* dubius, -a, -um	uncertain, doubtful
Ducenius, -i, m.	Ducenius
* dum	while, until, as long as
duo, -ae, -o	two
duoetvicensimus, -a, -um	twenty-second
duritia, -ae, f.	harshness
* dux, ducis, m.	general, leader
* e/ex (+ abl.)	from, out of, according to, for the advantage of
e contrario	on the contrary, instead
effero, efferare, efferavi, efferatum	make fierce
* effugio, effugere, effugi	flee
effugium, -i, n.	escape
effundo, effundere, effudi, effusum	squander
effusus, -a, -um	effusive
* ego, mei	I
* egredior, egredi, egressus sum	leave
egregius, -a, -um	excellent
elanguesco, elanguescere, elangui	grow weak
electio, -onis, f.	choice
eligo, eligere, elegi, electum	pick, choose, select
eludo, eludere, elusi, elusum	make light of
emetior, emitiri, emensus sum	measure out, pass through, live through
* emo, emere, emi, emptum	buy

* **enim**	for
enitor, eniti, enitus sum	struggle over
* **eo**	for this reason, therefore
* **eo, ire, ii (or ivi), itum**	go
* **eques, -itis, m.**	equestrian, knight
equester, -tris, -tre	equestrian
* **equus, -i, m.**	horse
* **erga (+ acc.)**	towards, with regard to
erigo, erigere, erexi, erectum	raise up
* **erro, errare, erravi, erratum**	stray, err, make a mistake
erumpo, erumpere, erupi, eruptum	burst out, break out
* **et**	and, also, even
et ipse	he also
* **etiam**	even, also
evenio, evenire, eveni, eventum	come out, happen
evenit (impersonal)	it happens
eventus, -us, m.	event, occurrence, outcome
everto, evertere, everti, eversum	overthrow
evocatus, -i, m.	veteran
evoco, evocare, evocavi, evocatum	call out, lure out
evulgo, evulgare, evulgavi, evulgatum	divulge
exactio, -onis, f.	collection (of money, taxes)
exarmo, exarmare, exarmavi, exarmatum	disarm
exauctoro, exauctorare, exauctoravi, exauctoratum	dismiss
* **excipio, excipere, excepi, exceptum**	take, receive
exclamo, exclamare, exclamavi, exclamatum	cry out
excuso, excusare, excusavi, excusatum	excuse
* **exemplum, -i, n.**	example, precedent
exerceo, exercere, exercui, exercitum	train, cultivate, exercise (power)
* **exercitus, -us, m.**	army
exhortatio, -onis, f.	exhortation
* **exilium, -i, n.**	exile
* **exitium, -i, n.**	destruction, ruin, end, death
exitus, -us, m.	end, result
exolvo, exolvere, exolvi, exolutum	pay

expectatio, -onis, f.	expectation
* **expecto, expectare, expectavi,** **expectatum**	wait for
experior, experiri, expertus sum	experience
exploro, explorare, exploravi, **exploratum**	examine
exposco, exposcere, expoposci	demanding
exprobro, exprobrare, exprobravi, **exprobratum**	reproach, denounce
exta, -orum, n. pl.	entrails
exterritus, -a, -um	terrified
extimulo, extimulare, extimulavi, **extimulatum**	spur on, incite
extra (+ acc.)	outside, free from
extremus, -a, -um	last
exul, -lis, m.	exile
exulto, exultare, exultavi	rejoice, triumph
Fabius, -i, m.	Fabius
* **facilis, -e**	easy, ready
facilitas, -atis, f.	ease, amiability, obligingness
* **facinus, -oris, n.**	crime
* **facio, facere, feci, factum**	make, do
factio, -onis, f.	faction, party
factum, -i, n.	deed
facultas, -atis, f.	opportunity
faenus, -oris, n.	capital
fallax, -acis	deceitful
* **fallo, fallere, fefelli, falsum**	deceive
falso	falsely
* **fama, -ae, f.**	talk, story, glory, reputation, rumour
* **familia, -ae, f.**	family
fas (indeclinable noun)	divine law, (often translated as adj.) right
fastidium, -i, n.	disgust, aversion
fatigo, fatigare, fatigavi, fatigatum	weary, harass
fatum, -i, n.	fate
* **faveo, favere, favi, fautum + dat.**	favour

favor, -oris, m.	favour, support, popularity
Februarius, -a, -um	of February
* felix, -icis	happy, fortunate
* femina, -ae, f.	woman
ferio, ferire	strike
feritas, -atis, f.	ferocity
ferme	almost
* fero, ferre, tuli, latum	carry, bear, tolerate, say
* ferox, -ocis	fierce
fessus, -a, -um	tired, weak
festinanter	hurriedly
festino, festinare, festinavi, festinatum	hurry, be in a hurry, act quickly
* fides, -ei, f.	credibility, loyalty
* fido, fidere, fisus sum	trust (+ dat.)
fidus, -a, -um	faithful
* filia, -ae, f.	daughter
fingo, fingere, finxi, finctum	invent, fabricate
* finis, -is, m.	end, death
* fio, fieri, factus sum	happen, become, be made (passive of *facio*)
firmo, firmare, firmavi, firmatum	strengthen
flagitium, -i, n.	disgrace, crime
flagito, flagitare, flagitavi, flagitatum	demand urgently, clamour for
flecto, flectere, flexi, flexum	bend, avert
floreo, florere, florui	flourish, be pre-eminent
Florus, -i, m.	Florus
fluctuo, fluctuare, fluctuavi, fluctuatum	swell, fluctuate
fluxus, -a, -um	weak
foedo, foedare, foedavi, foedatum	pollute
* foedus, -a, -um	shameful, foul, disgraceful, frightful
Fonteius, -i, m.	Fonteius
fore	= *futurum esse*
foris, -is, f.	door
forma, -ae, f.	form, shape, appearance, standard
formido, -inis, f.	fear
formidolosus, -a, -um	fearful, terrifying

fors, fortis, f.	fate, chance
* **forte**	by chance
* **fortis, -e**	brave
fortuitus, -a, -um	which happens by chance
* **fortuna, -ae, f.**	fortune, good luck
* **forum, -i, n.**	forum
foveo, fovere, fovi, fotum	cherish, favour, support
fremitus, -us, m.	roar
frequens, -entis	crowded
Fronto, -onis, m.	Fronto
* **frustra**	in vain
* **fuga, -ae, f.**	flight
fulgur, -uris, n.	lightning
furtim	in secret
futurum, i, n.	the future
futurus, -a, -um	future (or future participle of *sum*)
Galba, -ae, m.	Galba
Garutianus, -i, m.	Garutianus
* **gaudeo, gaudere, gavisus sum**	rejoice, be glad
* **gaudium, -i, n.**	joy, rejoicing
Geminus, -i, m.	Geminus
gener, -eri, m.	son-in-law
* **genus, -eris, n.**	kind, group, race
Germania, -ae, f.	Germany, one of the German provinces
Germanicus, -a, -um	German, in Germany
gesto, gestare, gestavi, gestatum	display
gigno, gignere, genui, genitus	bear; (in pass.) be born
* **gladius, -i, m.**	sword
gloria, -ae, f.	glory
glorior, gloriari, gloriatus sum	pride oneself in (+ abl.)
gradus, -us, m.	step
grandis, -e	great
* **gratia, -ae, f.**	favour, grace, influence
gratus, -a, -um	pleasing
* **gravis, -e**	serious
gregarius, -a, -um	common

* **habeo, habere, habui, habitum**	have, hold, employ, keep, consider
habitus, -us, m.	manner, bearing, dress, state
haesitatio, -onis, f.	hesitation
haruspex, -icis, m.	soothsayer
* **hasta, -ae, f.**	spear, auction
* **haud**	not
haud dubie	doubtlessly
haurio, haurire, hausi, haustum	draw (water), swallow, pierce
* **hic, haec, hoc**	this, he, she, it, the latter
hio, -are, -avi	gape, be eager
Hispania, -ae, f.	Spain
Hispanus, -a, -um	Spanish
* **hodie**	today
* **homo, -inis, m.**	man
honestus, -a, -um	honest, honourable, noble
* **honor, -oris, m.**	honour
honorificus, -a, -um	honour-bringing
hortus, -i, m.	garden
* **hostis, -is, m.**	enemy
* **huc**	to here, to this point
huc illuc	to and fro
humanus, a, um	human
humilis, -e	humble
* **iaceo, iacere, iacui, iacitum**	lie, be cast down
* **iacio, iacere, ieci, iactum**	throw
iacto, iactare, iactavi, iactatum	throw, boast
* **iam**	now, already
iam pridem	for a long time now
ianua, -ae, f.	door
Ianuarius, -a, -um	of January
* **ibi**	there
Icelus, -i, m.	Icelus
ictus, -us, m.	strike, blow
* **idem, eadem, idem**	the same, likewise
idem . . . qui	the same . . . as
idus, -uum, f. pl.	the Ides (13th or 15th day of the month)
* **igitur**	therefore

ignarus, -a, -um	ignorant, unaware, blind to (+ gen.)
ignavus, -a, -um	lazy, cowardly
* **ignoro, ignorare, ignoravi, ignoratum**	not know, be unacquainted with
ignotus, -a, -um	unknown
* **ille, illa, illum**	that, he, she, it, the former
illuc	to there
Illyricum, -i, n.	Illyricum
Illyricus, -a, -um	Illyrian
imago, -inis, f.	image, likenes, thought
imber, imbris, m.	rain
imbuo, imbuere, imbui, imbutum	drench, wet, steep
imitor, imitari, imitatus sum	act like
immensus, -a, -um	vast
immineo, imminere	hang over, loom over, threaten
immitis, -e	merciless
immodicus, -a, -um	unrestrained
impatiens, -entis	impatient
impello, impellere, impuli, impulsum	persuade, urge
impensus, -a, -um	excessive
* **imperator, -oris, m.**	emperor, general
imperatorius, -a, -um	of an emperor
imperitus, -a, -um	inexperienced
* **imperium, -i, n.**	power, imperial power, empire, discipline, rule
* **impero, imperare, imperavi, imperatum**	order (+ dat.), rule, be emperor
* **impetus, -us, m.**	attack, burst, impulsive action
impleo, implere, implevi, impletum	fill
impono, imponere, imposui, impositum	deceive, trick (+ dat.), place on (+ dat.)
imprimo, imprimere, impressi, impressum	drive in
impulsus, -us, m.	movement, instigation
* **in (+ abl.)**	in, on, at, in relation to, in the case of
* **in (+ acc.)**	into, against, to, in, for, for the sake of, between, towards, leading to
in dies	every day

in modum	in the manner
in posterum	for the future
inanis, -e	empty
inauditus, -a, -um	unheard, without a hearing
incautus, -a, -um	incautious
incertus, -a, -um	uncertain, doubtful
incessus, -us, m.	gait, way of walking
incido, incidere, incidi	encounter (with *in* + acc.)
* incipio, incipere, incepi, inceptum	begin
inclino, inclinare, inclinavi, inclinatum	incline, lean, dispose (a person or their mind)
inconstantia, -ae, f.	inconstancy
incorruptus, -a, -um	incorruptible
increpo, increpare, increpui, increpitum	reproach, criticize
incruentus, -a, -um	free from bloodshed
incuriosus	indifferent, neglectful, negligent
* inde	from there, then
indecorus, -a, -um	shameful
indefensus, -a, -um	undefended
indicium, -i, n.	sign, evidence
indignatio, -onis, f.	indignation
induco, inducere, induxi, inductum	lead in
inermis, -e	unarmed
inertia, -ae, f.	inactivity, laziness
infaustus, -a, -um	inauspicious
infelix, -icis	unlucky
infensus, -a, -um	hostile (+ dat.)
* infero, inferre, intuli, illatum	bring to
infestus, -a, -um	hostile
inficio, inficere, infeci, infectum	infect
infidus, -a, -um	untrustworthy
infirmus, -a, -um	weak
* ingenium, -i, n.	character, nature, inclination
* ingens, -entis	huge, plentiful
inimicus, -a, -um	hostile
* inimicus, -i, m.	enemy
* initium, -i, n.	beginning
inlaesus, -a, -um	unharmed

inmineo, -ere	see *immineo*
innitor, inniti, innixus sum	lean on, take the arm of (+ dat.)
innocens, -entis	innocent
* **inopia, -ae, f.**	poverty, lack, scarcity
inquietus, -a, -um	restless
* **inquit**	he/she/it says, said
inrisus, -us, m.	mockery, derision
inrumpo, inrumpere, inrupi, inruptum	burst into
inruo, inruere, inrui	rush in
insatiabilis, -e	insatiable
insero, inserere, inserui, insertum	introduce, drop in
* **insidiae, -arum, f. pl.**	traps, plot, treachery
* **insignis, -e**	distinguished, remarkable
insolitus, -a, -um	unusual
instinctor, -oris, m.	instigator, a person who urges on
insto, instare, institi	press upon, threaten, be imminent
instrumentum, -i, n.	tool, equipment
insuper	moreover, besides
integer, integra, integrum	whole, intact, untainted, honest
* **intellego, intellegere, intellexi, intellectum**	understand
intendo, intendere, intendi, intentum	extend, increase
intentus, -a, -um	intent upon (+ dat.)
* **inter (+ acc.)**	among, between
intercedo, intercedere, intercessi, intercessum	intervene, veto (+ dat.)
* **interea**	meanwhile
* **interficio, interficere, interfeci, interfectum**	kill
interim	meanwhile
interpretor, interpretari, interpretatus sum	interpret
interrogo, interrogare, interrogavi, interrogatum	ask
intersum, interesse, interfui	be present
interest (impersonal)	it concerns, it is important to (+ gen. or *mea, tua, sua* etc.)
intimus, -a, -um	most intimate, closest

intra (+ acc.)	within
intrepidus, -a, -um	undaunted
introitus, -us, m.	entrance
intueor, intueri, intuitus sum	look on
intus	inside
intutus, -a, -um	unsafe, dangerous
invado, invadere, invasi, invasum	invade, attack
invalidus, -a, -um	weak
* invenio, invenire, inveni, inventum	find
invidia, -ae, f.	unpopularity, hatred, jealousy
invidiosus, -a, -um	hatred-inducing
invisus, -a, -um	hated, unpopular
* ipse, ipsa, ipsum	himself, herself, itself, themselves
* ira, -ae, f.	anger
* iratus, -a, -um	angry
* is, ea, id	he, she, it, that, such
iste	that, he, she, it
* ita	thus, so, as follows, in such a way, nevertheless
* iter, itineris, n.	journey, way, march
* iubeo, iubere, iussi, iussum	order
iudicium, -i, n.	(sound) judgement, discernment
iugulum, -i, n.	throat
Iulius, -i, m.	Julius
ius, iuris, n.	law, (often translated as adj.) lawful
iussus, us, m.	command, order
iustitia, -ae, f.	justice
* iustus, -a, -um	just, fair
* iuvenis, -is, m.	young man
iuventa, -ae, f.	youth
* iuvo, iuvare, iuvavi, iuvatum	help
iuxta (+ acc.)	near to
iuxta (adverb)	close by
kalendae, -arum, f. pl.	Kalends (1st day of the month)
labo, labare, labavi	totter
* labor, -oris, m.	work, hardship

lacero, lacerare, laceravi, laceratum	mutilate
Laco, -onis, m.	Laco
lacus, -us, m.	lake
Laecanius, -i, m.	Laecanius
laetitia, -ae, f.	happiness
laetor, laetari, laetatus sum	be glad at (+ abl.)
* **laetus, -a, -um**	happy, pleasing, welcome, propitious
langueo, languere	weaken
lanio, laniare, laniavi, laniatum	mutilate
largitio, -onis, f.	bribery
latebra, -ae, f.	hiding place
* **latus, -a, -um**	wide, extensive
* **latus, -eris, n.**	side
* **laudo, laudare, laudavi, laudatum**	praise
* **laus, laudis, f.**	honour
legatio, -onis, f.	governorship
* **legatus, -i, m.**	commander, ambassador
* **legio, -onis, f.**	legion
legionarius, -a, -um	legionary
* **lego, legere, legi, lectum**	read, choose
lenocinium, -i, n.	flattery
levo, levare, levavi, levatum	lift up, lessen, alleviate
libellus, -i, m.	small book, document, petition
libenter	gladly, with pleasure
liberalitas, -atis, f.	generosity, gift
* **libertas, -atis, f.**	freedom, independence
Libertas, -atis, f.	Liberty
* **libertus, -i, m.**	freedman
libido, -inis, f.	desire, enjoyment, passion, lust, vice
licenter	freely, without restraint
licentia, -ae, f.	freedom, licence, lawlessness, lack of restraint
Licinianus, -i, m.	Licinianus
limen, -inis, n.	threshold
lingua, -ae, f.	tongue
* **litterae, -arum, f. pl**	letter
lixa, -ae, m.	camp-follower
* **locus, -i, m.**	place, room, opportunity

Longinus, -i, m.	Longinus
* **longus, -a, -um**	long, long-standing
* **loquor, loqui, locutus sum**	say, speak
ludibrium, -i, n.	insult
ludicrum, -i, n.	spectacle
lugubris, -e	sad, grim
Lusitania, -ae, f.	Lusitania
luxuria, -ae, f.	extravagance
luxus, -us, m.	luxury, excess
M.	Marcus
Macer, Macri, m.	Macer
maculosus, -a, -um	stained, defiled
maestitia, -ae, f.	sadness
maestus, -a, -um	sad, downcast
magis	more, rather
magnitudo, -inis, f.	size
* **magnus, -a, -um**	big, great, important
maiestas, -atis, f.	imperial majesty
maior, -ius	greater (comparative of *magnus*)
malum, -i, n.	evil, harm
* **malus, -a, -um**	bad, wicked
* **mando, mandare, mandavi, mandatum**	order
* **maneo, manere, mansi, mansum**	stay, remain, wait for, be fixed
manifestus, -a, -um	clear
* **manus, -us, f.**	hand
Marcianus, -i, m.	Macianus
Marius, -i, m.	Marius
Martialis, -is, m.	Martialis
materia, -ae, f.	material, fuel
mathematicus, -i, m.	astrologer
matrimonium, -i, n.	marriage
maturo, maturare, maturavi, maturatum	ripen, hasten
* **medius, -a, -um**	(in the) middle, intervening, indifferent, middling
melior, -ius	better (comparative of *bonus*)
memorabilis, -e	memorable

memoria, -ae, f.	memory
mendacium, -i, n.	lies
* mens, mentis, f.	mind, feeling
mensis, -is, m.	month
mereo, merere, merui, meritum	deserve
mereor, mereri, meritus sum	deserve
merito	deservingly
meritum, -i, n.	service
metuo, metuere, metui, metutum	fear
* metus, -us, m.	fear
* meus, -a, -um	my
* miles, -itis, m.	soldier, soldiery
miliarium, -i, n.	milestone
miliens	a thousand times
militaris, -e	military, of (the) soldiers
militia, -ae, f.	military service
mille (indeclinable); (in pl.) milia, -ium, n. pl.	thousand
minaciter	with threats
minae, -arum, f. pl.	threats
* minor, minari, minatus sum	threaten
minor, -us	less, smaller, less important
miraculum, -i, n.	wonder
misceo, miscere, miscui, mixtum	mix in
* miser, -era, -erum	miserable, wretched
misericordia, -ae, f.	pity
missus, -us, m.	sending
* mitto, mittere, misi, missum	send
mobilitas, -atis, f.	mobility, fickleness
moderate	with moderation
moderatus, -a, -um	moderate, modest
modestia, -ae, f.	modesty, self-restraint
* modo	only
modo . . . modo	now . . . now
* modus, -i, m.	way, manner, type, end
molior, moliri, molitus sum	strive for
mollis, -e	soft, lenient, effeminate
monitus, -us, m.	warning, advice
* mora, -ae, f.	delay

* **mors, mortis, f.**	death
mortalis, -e	mortal
* **mos, moris, m.**	custom, habit, manner, style, (pl.) character
motus, -us, m.	movement, change, agitation, uprising, emotion
* **moveo, movere, movi, motum**	disturb
* **mox**	soon
mucro, -onis, m.	sword
mulceo, mulcere, mulsi, mulsum	appease
muliebris, -e	womanly
* **multitudo, -inis, f.**	large number, mob
* **multus, -a, -um**	much, many
munimentum, -i, n.	protection
Murcus, -i, m.	Murcus
* **muto, mutare, mutavi, mutatum**	change
mutuus, -a, -um	mutual
* **nam**	for
Naso, -onis, m.	Naso
natales, -ium, m. pl.	family, lineage
* **natura, -ae, f.**	nature
navigatio, -onis, f.	voyage
* **ne**	lest, so that ... not, not ... to, that ... not
* **-ne**	marks a yes/no question
-ne ... an ...	whether ... or
ne ... quidem	not even
* **nec**	see *neque*
necdum	not yet
* **necesse**	necessary
necessitas, -atis, f.	necessity, obligation
* **neglego, neglegere, neglexi, neglectum**	neglect
* **nemo, nullius**	no one
* **neque**	and ... not, also ... not
neque ... neque	neither ... nor
nequeo, nequire, nequivi, nequitum	not be able, be unable
Nero, -onis, m.	Nero
Neronianus, -a, -um	of, concerning Nero

* **nescio, nescire, nescivi, nescitum**   not know
ni   = *nisi*
* **nihil**   nothing, (adverbially) not at all
nimirum   doubtless
nimius, -a, -um   excessive, immoderate
* **nisi**   if ... not
* **nobilis, -e**   noble
nobilitas, -atis, f.   nobility
nocens, entis   guilty
* **noceo, nocere, nocui**   harm, ruin (+ dat.)
* **nolo, nolle, nolui**   not want, be unwilling
* **nomen, -inis, n.**   name, account, title
nominatim   specifically
nomino, nominare, nominavi,   name
    nominatum
* **non**   not
* **nondum**   not yet
* **nos, nostri (nostrum)**   we
* **noster, nostra, nostrum**   our
notabils, -e   notable
novum, -i, n.   news
* **novus, -a, -um**   new
    novae res   revolution
    novi motus   revolution
* **nox, noctis, f.**   night
* **nullus, -a, -um**   no, not any
* **num**   whether
* **numerus, -i, m.**   number, detachment
* **nunc**   now
nuncupo, noncupare, noncupavi,   proclaim
    noncupatum
* **nuntio, nuntiare, nuntiavi, nuntiatum**   announce
* **nuntius, -i, m.**   messenger, message, report, news
nuper   recently
nuto, nutare, nutavi, nutatum   waver, hesitate
Nymphidius, -i, m.   Nymphidius

* **ob (+ acc.)**   for, because of
oblivio, -onis, f.   oblivion, forgetting

* obliviscor, oblivisci, oblitus sum	forget (+ gen.)
obscurus, -a, -um	mysterious
obsequium, -i, n.	compliance, subservience
observatio, -onis, f.	observation
observo, observare, observavi, observatum	observe
obsidio, -onis, f.	seige
obtentus, -us, m.	covering, veil
obvius, -a, -um	in one's way, ready
obvius sum (+ dat.)	meet, encounter
* occido, occidere, occidi, occisum	kill
* occupo, occupare, occupavi, occupatum	seize, forestall
occurro, occurrere, occurri, occursum	run to meet, rush against (+ dat.)
Octavia, -ae, f.	Octavia
octavus, -a, -um	eighth
oculus, -i, m.	eye
* odium, -i, n.	hatred
* offero, offerre, obtuli, oblatum	offer, (in passive + dat.) encounter
* officium, -i, n.	duty
* olim	once
omen, -inis, n.	omen, sign
* omnis, -e	all, every
onero, onerare, oneravi, oneratum	weigh down
onerosus, -a, -um	onerous
Onomastus, -i, m.	Onomastus
* opera, -ae, f.	deed
oppono, opponere, opposui, oppositum	put in the way, deploy
* opportunus, -a, -um	opportune
* opprimo, opprimere, oppressi, oppressum	crush, overwhelm
* ops, opis, f.	power, assistance, (pl.) wealth
* optimus, -a, -um	best (superlative of *magnus*)
opto, optare, optavi, optatum	desire
* opus, -eris, n.	work
* *opus est*	there is need of (+ abl.)
* oratio, -onis, f.	speech, oration
* ordo, -inis, m.	rank

* **orior, oriri, ortus sum**	arise
ornatus, -us, m.	dress, attire
osculum, -i, n.	kiss
ostento, ostentare, ostentavi, ostentatum	show, present, exhibit, hold out the prospect of
Otho, -onis, m.	Otho
Othonianus, -i, m.	supporter of Otho
Pacensis, -is, m.	Pacensis
Pacorus, -i, m.	Pacorus
paenitentia, -ae, f.	repentance
paeniteo, paenitere, paenitui	displease, cause to regret
paenitet (impersonal)	it is a cause of regret
Palatium, -i, n.	the Palatine, the palace
Pannonicus, -a, -um	Pannonian, from Pannonia
* **par, paris**	equal, the same, measuring up
paratus, -a, -um	ready, available
paratus, -us, m.	preparation
parcus, -a, -um	sparing, stingy
* **paro, parare, paravi, paratum**	prepare
* **pars, partis, f.**	part, (pl.) faction
* **pater, patris, m.**	father, (pl.) senators
patiens, -entis	patient, tolerant
* **patior, pati, passus sum**	suffer, allow, acquiesce
Patrobius, -i, m.	Patrobius
* **pauci, -ae, -a**	few
paucitas, -atis, f.	small number, scantiness
* **paulo**	a little
* **pauper, -eris**	poor
paveo, -ere	fear
* **pax, pacis, f.**	peace
pecco, peccare, peccavi, peccatum	do wrong, sin
pectus, -oris, n.	chest
* **pecunia, -ae, f.**	money
* **pello, pellere, pepuli, pulsum**	drive out
penes (+ acc.)	in the hands of, under the control of
* **per (+ acc.)**	through, throughout, during, (of time) for, by
percussor, -oris, m.	assassin, murderer

perditus, -a, -um	depraved
* **perdo, perdere, perdidi, perditum**	lose, ruin
* **pereo, perire, perii, peritum**	perish, die
pergo, pergere, perrexi, perrectum	proceed, continue
* **periculum, -i, n,**	danger
peritia, -ae, f.	skill
* **peritus, -a, -um**	skilled, expert
perlustro, perlustrare, perlustravi, perlustratum	scrutinize
* **permitto, permittere, permisi, permissum**	permit, entrust, allow, grant
perniciosus, -a, -um	destructive
* **persuadeo, persuadere, persuasi, persuasum**	persuade (+ dat.)
pertempto, pertemptare, pertemptavi, pertemptatum	test
pertinacia, -ae, f.	persistence
pertineo, pertinere, pertinui	relate
pervado, pervadere, pervasi, pervasum	make one's way
pervicax, -acis	stubborn
* **pessimus, -a, -um**	very bad (superlative of *malus*)
* **peto, petere, petivi, petitum**	make for
Petronius, -i, m.	Petronius
petulanter	insolently, shamelessly
* **pilum, -i, n.**	javelin
Piso, -onis, m.	Piso
placatus, -a, -um	well-disposed
* **placeo, placere, placui, placitum**	please (+ dat.)
placet (impersonal)	it is decided
plausus, -us, m.	applause
Plautus, -i, m.	Plautus
* **plebs, plebis, f.**	plebs, populace, mob
* **plenus, -a, -um**	full
* **plerique, pleraeque, pleraque**	most, very many, the majority
* **plurimus, -a, -um**	most, very many (superlative of *multus*)
plurimum (adverb)	the most
* **plus, pluris**	more (comparative of *multus*)

* poena, -ae, f.	punishment
Pompeius, -i, m.	Pompeius
* pono, ponere, posui, positum	place, put aside
poples, -itis, m.	back of the knee
Poppaea, -ae, f.	Poppaea
* populus, -i, m.	people
porticus, -us, f.	colonnade
portio, -onis, f.	share, portion
* posco, poscere, poposci	demand
* possum, posse, potui	can, be able
* post (+ acc.)	after
* post (adverb)	after
* postea	afterwards
posteri, -orum, m.	future generations
posterus, -a, -um	next, following, future
* postquam	after
* postremus, -a, -um	final
* postulo, postulare, postulavi, postulatum	demand
* potens, -entis	powerful
potentia, -ae, f.	power
* potestas, -atis, f.	power
* potius	rather, instead
* praebeo, praebere, praebui, praebitum	provide
praeceps, -ipitis	headlong, at a rush
praecipio, praecipere, praecepi, praeceptum	order
praeclarus, -a, -um	remarkable
praedico, praedicere, praedixi, praedictum	predict, foretell, proclaim
praedium, -i, n.	property
praeeo, praeire, praeii (or -ivi), praeitum	recite
praefectus, -i, m.	prefect
praefigo, praefigere, praefixi, praefixum	fix on (+ dat.)
praefor, praefari, praefatus sum	say first
praegravis, -e	very heavy, very troublesome

praemitto, praemittere, praemisi, praemissum	send ahead, send forth
* **praemium, -i, n.**	reward
praepono, praeponere, praeposui, praepositum	put in charge of (+ dat.)
praepositus, -i, m.	officer
praepotens, -entis	very powerful
praeripio, praeripere, praeripui, praereptum	snatch away
praesens, -entis	present
praetextus, -us, m.	display
praetorianus, -a, -um	praetorian
praetorium, -i, n.	Praetorian Guard
praetorius, -a, -um	praetorian
praevenio, praevenire, praeveni, praeventum	anticipate, forestall
prenso, prensare, prensavi, prensatum	grasp
* **pretium, -i, n.**	price, gift
pridem	long ago, for a long time
primipilaris, -is, m.	ex-primus pilus (centurion of the first rank)
primo	at first
primoris, -e	leading, foremost
primum	at first
* **primus, -a, -um**	first, initial
* **princeps, -ipis, m.**	emperor, princeps
principalis, -e	imperial
principatus, -us, m.	principate, empire, imperial power
* **prior, -ius**	first, former, past
privatus, -a, -um	private, personal
privatus, -i, m.	private citizen, person without public office
* **pro (+ abl.)**	in front of, on behalf of, for, instead of, in place of, for the sake of
pro consule (or proconsul)	pro consul
proclamo, proclamare, proclamavi, proclamatum	proclaim

proculco, proculcare, proculcavi, proculcatum	trample down
procurator, -oris, m.	procurator
prodigo, prodigere, prodegi	squander
* **prodo, prodere, prodidi, proditum**	hand down, report, reveal, betray
* **proficiscor, proficisci, profectus sum**	set out
proicio, proicere, proieci, proiectum	throw down
proinde	therefore, just as much
* **promitto, promittere, promisi, promissum**	promise
pronuntio, pronuntiare, pronuntiavi, pronuntiatum	announce
pronus, -a, -um	inclined, disposed
Propinquus, -i, m.	Propinquus
proprius, -a, -um	his own, her own, their own
prospecto, prospectare, prospectavi, prospectatum	look out
prospectus, -us, m.	sight, view
prosperus, -a, -um	favourable
protendo, protendere, protendi, protentum	stretch out
protraho, protrahere, protraxi, protractum	drag out
proturbo, proturbare, proturbavi, proturbatum	drive away
prout	in so far as, depending on
provideo, providere, providi, provisum	foresee, (with ut-clause) see to it that
* **provincia, -ae, f.**	province
provolvo, provolvere, provolvi, provolutum	roll something forward, (in passive) roll forward
* **proximus, -a, -um**	nearest, most recent, next, (+ dat.) closest to
proximus, i, m.	associate, intimate
Ptolemaeus, -i, m.	Ptolemaeus
publicae	state
publicum, -i, n.	public
* **publicus, -a, -um**	public, of the people, of the state

pueritia, -ae, f.	boyhood
pugio, -onis, m.	dagger
pulcher, -chra, -chrum	glorious
* **punio, punire, punivi, punitum**	punish
* **puto, putare, putavi, putatum**	think, consider
Pyrenaeus, -i, m.	Pyrenees
quadriduum, -i, n.	(period of) four days
quaero, quaerere, quaesivi, quaesitum	seek, gain
* **qualis, -e**	of the sort which
* **quam**	than, as
* **quamquam**	although
quamvis	although, however
quantuluscumque, -acumque, -umcumque	however little, very little
quantus, -a, -um	how much, to which extent
quartus, -a, -um	fourth
* **quasi**	as if
quattuordecim	fourteen
* **-que**	and
querela, -ae, f.	complaint
* **queror, queri, questus sum**	complaning
* **qui, quae, quod**	who, which (and as connecting relative)
* **quia**	since, because
quicumque, quaecumque, quodcumque	whatever, any
* **quidam, quaedam, quoddam**	a certain, (in pl.) some
* **quidem**	indeed
* **quies, -etis, f.**	quiet, inaction
quiesco, quiescere, quievi, quietum	rest, keep quiet, be inactive
quinque	five
quintus decimus, -a, -um	fifteenth
quippe	indeed, since
* **quis, quid**	who, which
* **quisque, quaeque, quodque**	each, every, (+ superlative) all the most . . .
* **quisquis, quidquid**	whoever, whatever

quo	so that (when purpose clause contains a comparative)
quo minus	from (introduces a clause of hindering or prevention)
* **quod**	because, on the grounds that
quonam	to where exactly, how far exactly
* **quoque**	also
rapax, -acis	greedy
rapidus, -a, -um	quick
* **rapio, rapere, rapui, raptum**	seize, snatch, grasp, carry off (to declare as emperor)
* **ratio, -onis, f.**	reason
* **recens, -entis**	fresh
recordatio, -onis, f.	recollection
rectus, -a, -um	correct, fair
redemptor, -oris, m.	contractor
* **redeo, redire, redii, reditum**	return
* **refero, referre, rettuli, relatum**	bring back
refoveo, refovere, refovi, refotum	restore (to health)
refringo, refringere, refregi, refractum	break down
* **regnum, -i, n.**	royal power, kingdom
regressus, -us, m.	retreat
relatus, -us, m.	account
religio, -onis, f.	sancitity
* **relinquo, relinquere, reliqui, relictum**	leave
remaneo, remanere, remansi	remain, stay
remedium, -i, n.	remedy, cure
reor, reri, ratus sum	think, regard
repens, -entis	sudden
reperio, reperire, repperi, repertum	find
repeto, repetere, repetivi, repetitum	seek
reprehensio, -onis, f.	finding fault, criticism
repugno, repugnare, repugnavi, repugnatum	fight back, oppose (+ dat.)
requiro, requirere, requisivi, requisitum	ask, ask after

* **res, rei, f.**	thing, affair, event, matter, situation, condition, government
res novae	revolution
* ***res publica***	state, republic
* **resisto, resistere, restiti**	resist (+ dat.)
resono, resonare, resonavi	resound
* **respondeo, respondere, respondi, responsum**	reply
* **retineo, retinere, retinui, retentum**	retain
reverens, -entis	respectful
reverentia, -ae, f.	respect, regard
revoco, revocare, revocavi, revocatum	recall
rigor, -oris, m.	stiffness, inflexibility
Romanus, -a, -um	Roman, of Rome
Roma, -ae, f.	Rome
rostra, -orum, n. pl.	the Rostra
Rubellius, -i, m.	Rubellius
rubor, -oris, m.	shame
rumor, -oris, m.	rumour, report, gossip
* **rumpo, rumpere, rupi, ruptum**	break
ruo, ruere, rui	rush, burst
* **rursus**	again
Sabina, -ae, f.	Sabina
Sabinus, -i, m.	Sabinus
sacramentum, -i, n.	oath
sacrifico, sacrificare, sacrificavi, sacrificatum	sacrifice
sacrum, -i, n.	religious observance, rite
* **saepe**	often
saevitia, -ae, f.	savagery
* **saluto, salutare, salutavi, salutatum**	greet
sane	indeed, certainly
* **sanguis, -inis, m.**	blood
* **sapientia, -ae, f.**	wisdom
* **satis**	enough
Saturnus, -i, m.	Saturn
* **scelus, -eris, n.**	crime

scindo, scindere, scidi, scissum	divide, separate
* **scio, scire, scivi, scitum**	know, know how to
scortum, -i, n.	whore
Scribonia, -ae, f.	Scribonia
scrutor, scrutari, scrutatus sum	investigate, scrutinize
* **se, sui**	himself, herself, itself, themselves
secreto	in secret
secretum, -i, n.	secret, secret dealing
sector, -oris, m.	speculator
* **secundus, -a, -um**	favourable
* **sed**	but
seditio, -onis, f.	revolt, rebellion
segnis, -e	lazy, inactive
segnitia, -ae, f.	inactivity
sella, -ae, f.	chair
* **semel**	once
* **semper**	always
Sempronius, -i, m.	Sempronius
* **senator, -oris, m.**	senator
* **senatus, -us, m.**	senate
senectus, -utis, f.	old age
senex, -is (adjective)	old
* **senex, -is, m.**	old man
senior, -oris, m.	an older man
senium, -i, n.	old age
* **sententia, -ae, f.**	opinion, feeling, idea, advice
sepono, seponere, seposui, sepositum	banish
septuaginta	seventy
sepultura, -ae, f.	burial
* **sequor, sequi, secutus sum**	follow
Serenus, -i, m.	Serenus
sermo, -onis, m.	conversation, speech, word, remark
serviliter	like a slave
servitium, -i, m.	slavery, group of slaves, a slave
Servius, -i, m.	Servius
* **servo, servare, servavi, servatum**	keep
* **servus, -i, m.**	slave
sestertium, -i, n.	a hundred thousand sesterces

set	= *sed*
* seu	= *sive*
severitas, -atis, f.	severity, strictness
severus, -a, -um	strict, stern
Severus, -i, m.	Severus
sextus, -a, -um	sixth
* si	if, to see if
sidus, -eris, n.	star
significatio, -onis, f.	sign
significo, significare, significavi, significatum	reveal
* signum, -i, n.	sign, standard
* silentium, -i, n.	silence
* similis, -e	similar, like (+ gen. or dat.)
* simul	at the same time, and also
simulatio, -onis, f.	pretence
* sine (+ abl.)	without
singuli, -ae, -a	individual, each, one-by-one
* sinister, -tra, -trum	left, unfavourable
* sive	or if
sive . . . sive	either . . . or, whether . . . or
sobrius, -a, -um	sober
socer, -eri, m.	father-in-law
* socius, -i, m.	ally
solacium, -i, n.	solace
* soleo, solere, solitus sum	accustomed
solitum, -i, n.	the customary, what is usual
solium, -i, n.	seat, throne
sollicitudo, -inis, f.	anxiety
sollicitus, -a, -um	anxious
solum, -i, n.	ground
* solus, -a, -um	alone, only
sordidus, -a, -um	dirty, base, disgraceful
spargo, spargere, sparsi, sparsum	scatter
* spatium, -i, n.	space, expanse, distance, time
species, -ei, f.	appearance, pretext, guise
speciosus, -a, -um	attractive, specious
speculator, -oris, m.	bodyguard, member of the bodyguard

* sperno, spernere, sprevi, spretum	scorn
* spero, sperare, speravi, speratum	hope, have hopes
* spes, -ei, f.	hope
splendidus, -a, -um	bright, distinguished
* statim	immediately, at once, on the spot
statio, -onis, f.	guard duty, post
stationem ago	keep guard, be on guard duty
Statius, -i, m.	Statius
statua, -ae, f.	statue
stimulo, stimulare, stimulavi, stimulatum	goad
strepo, strepere, strepui, strepitum	resound
stringo, stringere, strixi, strictum	draw (a weapon)
* studium, -i, n.	passion, zeal, enthusiasm, support
* stultus, -a, -um	stupid, foolish
stuprum, -i, n.	disgrace
suadeo, suadere, suasi, suasum	urge, recommend
* sub (+ acc. or abl.)	under
subeo, subire, subii, subitum	approach, enter, influence (of emotions, etc.)
subitum, -i, n.	unexpected occurrence
subitus, -a, -um	sudden
Subrius, -i, m.	Subrius
substituo, substituere, substitui, substitutum	substitute
succedo, succedere, successi, successum	succeed
successio, -onis, f.	succession
successor, -oris, m.	successor
suetus, -a, -um	accustomed (+ dat.)
suffigo, suffigere, suffixi, suffixum	fix, impale
suggestus, -us, m.	platform
Sulpicius, -i, m.	Sulpicius
* sum, esse, fui	be
* sumo, sumere, sumpsi, sumptum	take up
sumptus, -us, m.	spending, extravagance
super (+ acc.)	besides
superior, -ius	upper

* **supersum, superesse, superfui**	remain, be left over, survive (+ dat.)
suppliciter	like a suppliant
supprimo, supprimere, suppressi, suppressum	suppress
suspectus, -a, -um	mistrusted, suspicious, suspect
suspicio, suspicere, suspexi, suspectum	suspect
suspicio, -onis, f.	suspicion
* **suus, -a, -um**	his, her, its, their (own)
tabes, -is, f.	disease
* **talis, -e**	such, of such a kind
* **tam**	so, as
tam . . . quam	as . . . as
non tam . . . quam	not so much . . . as
* **tamen**	however, yet
tamquam	just as, as if, as happens, (+ subjunctive) on the grounds that
* **tantum**	only
* **tantus, -a, -um**	so great, such a great
tardus, -a, -um	slow
Taurus, -i, m.	Taurus
* **tego, tegere, texi, tectum**	protect
* **telum, -i, n.**	weapons
temeritas, -atis, f.	rashness
* **templum, -i, n.**	temple
* **tempus, -oris, n.**	time
temulentus, -a, -um	drunk
tendo, tendere, tetendi, tentum	stretch, strain, exert oneself, be encamped
tenebrae, -arum, f. pl.	shadows, darkness
tenus (postposed + abl.)	to the extent of
Terentius, -i, m.	Terentius
tero, terere, trivi, tritum	rub, waste
* **terreo, terrere, terrui, territum**	frighten, deter
theatrum, -i, n.	theatre
thorax, -acis, m.	breastplate

Tiberianus, -a, -um	of Tiberius
* timeo, timere, timui	fear
Titus, -i, m.	Titus
tolero, tolerare, toleravi, toleratum	bear, endure
tonitruum, -i, n.	thunder
* tot	so many
totidem	the same number
* totus, -a, -um	whole
* trado, tradere, tradidi, traditum	hand over, relate, hand down
traduco, traducere, traduxi, traductum	lead over, bring over
transcendo, transcendere, transcendi, transcensum	pass
transeo, transire, transii (or -ivi), transitum	cross
transfero, transferre, transtuli, translatum	transfer, remove
transfuga, -ae, m.	runaway
transgredior, transgredi, transgressus sum	go over
transigo, transigere, transegi, transactum	carry out, conduct
transitus, -us, m.	passing, change
transmitto, transmittere, transmisi, transmissum	pass over
transverbero, transverberare, transverberavi, transverberatum	pierce through
Trebonius, -i, m.	Trebonius
trepidatio, -onis, f.	panic
trepido, trepidare, trepidavi, trepidatum	be alarmed
trepidus, -a, -um	anxious, panic-stricken
tres, tria	three
tribunus, -i, m.	tribune
triginta	thirty
* tristis, -e	sad, ill-humoured, unfavourable, unfortunate

trucido, trucidare, trucidavi, trucidatum	slaughter, massacre
truncus, -a, -um	maimed
trux, -cis	harsh, ferocious
* **tum**	then
* **tumultus, -us, m.**	tumult, uproar
tumulus, -i, m.	mound, tomb
* **turba, -ae, f.**	crowd
turbamentum, -i, n.	means of disturbing
turbidus, -a, -um	turbulent, confused
turbo, turbare, turbavi, turbatum	disturb, upset, make trouble
Turpilianus, -i, m.	Turpilianus
* **ubi**	when
* **ubique**	everywhere
* **ullus, -a, -um**	any
ultio, -onis, f.	vengeance
ultor, -oris, m.	avenger
ultra (+ acc.)	beyond
ultro	furthermore, even, of one's own accord
Umbricius, -i, m.	Umbricius
* **umquam**	ever
* **undique**	everywhere
unicus, -a, -um	one and only
universus, -a, -um	whole (of)
unus, -a, -um	one
urbanus, -a, -um	urban, city
* **urbs, urbis, f.**	city
urgeo, urgere, ursi	urge
* **usque**	all the way
usurpo, usurpare, usurpavi, usurpatum	acquire, make use of, enjoy
* **ut**	as, when, because, on the grounds of, as is natural, as if, depending on, that, so that
ut qui	because (causal relative)
ut quisque	whenever anyone, whoever
ut . . . ita	although . . . nevertheless
* **uterque, utraque, utrumque**	both

utrimque	on both sides
* **uxor, -oris, f.**	wife
vaco, vacare, vacavi, vacatum	be free for, be open to (+ dat.)
vacuus, -a, -um	empty
vagus, -a, -um	vague
Valens, -entis, m.	Valens
* **valeo, valere, valui, valitum**	be strong
valesco, valescere	grow strong
vallum, -i, n.	fortification
varie	in different ways
varius, -a, -um	varied
Varro, -onis, m.	Varro
* **-ve**	or
* **vel**	or, even
Velabrum, -i, n.	the Velabrum
venalis, -e	for sale
venditator, -oris, m.	boaster
* **verbum, -i, n.**	word
vere	truly
vereor, vereri, veritus sum	fear, respect
Vergilio, -onis, m.	Vergilio
veritas, -atis, f.	integrity
* **vero**	indeed, in truth
* **verto, vertere, verti, versum**	turn
verum, -i, n.	truth
Vesta, -ae, f.	Vesta
* **vester, vestra, vestrum**	your
* **veto, vetare, vetavi, vetatum**	forbid
* **vetus, -eris**	old, ancient
vetustas, -atis, f.	age
vetustus, -a, -um	old, long-serving
vexilla, -ae, f.	military ensign, detachment
vexillarius, -i, m.	standard-bearer
vexo, vexare, vexavi, vexatum	maltreat
* **via, -ae, f.**	road
vicem (adverb)	for the sake of (+ gen.)
viciens	twenty times
* **video, videre, vidi, visum**	see

* videor, videri, visus sum	seem
viduus, -a, -um	unmarried
vigeo, -ere, -ui	be vigorous, bloom
vigil, -ilis, m.	guard, (pl.) city watch
viginti	twenty
* vinco, vincere, vici, victum	beat, conquer
Vindex, -icis, m.	Vindex
Vinius, -i, m.	Vinius
Vipsanius, -a, -um	Vispanian, of Vipsanius
* vir, viri, m.	man
* virtus, -utis, f.	virtue
* vis, vim (acc.), vi (abl.), vires (nom. pl.), f.	force, violence, (pl.) strength, power
* vita, -ae, f.	life
Vitellius, -i, m.	Vitellius
vitium, -i, n.	fault, sin, vice
* vito, vitare, vitavi, vitatum	avoid
* vix	scarcely
vixdum	scarcely
vocito, vocitare, vocitavi, vocitatum	call often, be accustomed to call
* voco, vocare, vocavi, vocatum	call
* volo, velle, volui	want
Vologaesus, -i, m.	Vologaesus
voluntas, -atis, f.	wish, free will
voluptas, -atis, f.	pleasure, enjoyment
volvo, volvere, volvi, volutum	turn over
* vos, vestri (vestrum)	you
votum, -i, n.	wish, longing
* vox, -vocis, f.	voice, speech, cry, saying
vulgo, vulgare, vulgavi, vulgatum	spread
vulgus, -i, n. or m.	common people, common soldiers, rabble
* vulnero, vulnerare, vulneravi, vulneratum	wound
* vulnus, -eris, n.	wound
* vultus, -us, m.	face, look, expression

28479012R00111

Printed in Great Britain
by Amazon